ALCOHOL RECOVERY

G000160841

A Self-help Guide to Get Free From Alcoholism

(Stop Your Drinking With Alcohol Treatment and Recovery Help)

Laurie Segura

Published by Tomas Edwards

© **Laurie Segura**

All Rights Reserved

Alcohol Recovery: A Self-help Guide to Get Free From Alcoholism (Stop Your Drinking With Alcohol Treatment and Recovery Help)

ISBN 978-1-990373-34-3

Legal & Disclaimer

The information contained in this book is not designed to replace or take the place of any form of medicine or professional medical advice. The information in this book has been provided for educational and entertainment purposes only.

The information contained in this book has been compiled from sources deemed reliable, and it is accurate to the best of the Author's knowledge; however, the Author cannot guarantee its accuracy and validity and cannot be held liable for any errors or omissions. Changes are periodically made to this book. You must consult your doctor or get professional medical advice before using any of the

Table of Contents

Introduction

It is great having you here read this book. I don't care if it's for yourself or somebody you care about – looking for a solution is always the first step to a brighter future. The problem of alcohol addiction is a very serious one worldwide and many people are suffering from it. You may be too, or you may be looking for information for a friend. Whichever the case may be, it is hoped that you will find sufficient information within the pages of this book to actually do something about it.

You have to remember that the first step to curing alcohol addiction is actually admitting that there is a problem. When people around you are suffering, it's even more important because you can lose your livelihood and you can lose friendships and relationships that you may have counted on as long as you remember. The reason? Alcohol is the reason. It makes you unreasonable and difficult to befriend.

With the advice found in this book, you should be able to decide if this applies to you and then do something positive to make a difference to your life.

Chapter 1: Stop Drinking!

Alcohol addiction is not new. Because of certain circumstances in life, people become addicted to alcohol and this addiction has somehow affected their daily lives. Some rely on alcohol to forget their problems while others drink to gain instant confidence. Still others claim to drink occasionally while actually they look for an occasion as an excuse to drink. But no matter what the reason has made a person dependent on alcohol, *this addiction has to stop*. It is not easy to overcome addiction especially from alcohol especially if drinking has become your only source of reason in life.

If you:

- Have suffered from an accident or have been arrested due to drunk driving

-problems in your relationships due to drinking alcohol

- Have problems with your job, school or career because of drinking alcohol

- Have problems with finances due to drinking alcohol

- Have suffered from health issues due to alcohol

- Have felt depressed and stressed because of drinking alcohol

- Would like to start a brand new life without alcohol

Then this guide is for YOU!

Just like in any addiction recovery program, accepting that you have a problem and that you need help is the first step to recovery. Being in denial will never get you anywhere. You need to have the guts to stand up for yourself and fight addiction. YES, YOU CAN!

WARNING:

It is not easy to quit alcohol. A lot of people that wanted to quit, quit trying after a week. However, if you quit now, what will you achieve? You will only end up going through the same troubles again and start feeling sorry and depressed once more.

For heavy drinkers, there is a certain period called the *Withdrawal Phase* in an alcohol recovery program. The withdrawal phase is when you will feel uncomfortable symptoms as the alcohol leaves your system completely. This is another reason why most people that would like to stop drinking start to take alcohol again.

This phase is just a stage in your recovery. Everyone pulls through and it is a guarantee that after alcohol has completely left your system, you will feel a lot better. The withdrawal phase could last a week or two weeks depending on how severe the person's addiction to alcohol.

You must have a strong support system during your recovery from alcohol. Yes you can do this alone but having someone you trust be with you makes a huge difference!

You must seek professional help if you have medical conditions or if you think that you need a professional guide to help you recover from alcohol addiction.

You must think positively! Positive thinking allows you to focus and achieve your goals.

Chapter 2: Alcoholism Recovery

It is easier to develop an addiction to alcohol than it is to recover from alcoholism. Understanding and accepting this, is among the many first steps towards a successful journey towards recovery from alcohol addiction.

There are many obstacles that can actually prevent a person from successfully recovering from alcohol addiction, and you might be surprised to know some of these hurdles.

Obstacle 1: Believing that recovery from alcoholism is easy

Through hindsight, it may seem much easier. However while you are going through the fight against alcohol addiction, it will feel like one of the hardest things you have ever had to face. For that matter, it probably is. There is more to recovering from alcohol dependency than just quitting drinking. You may have heard that a recovering alcoholic is always a recovering alcoholic, and that is because recovery is a journey without end.

Overcoming this obstacle:

Before you can fight alcoholism, and win, you have to be prepared to fight. In order to do this, you have to have a full understanding of what you are up against. With the right motivation, it can be easy to make it through each day, taking one step at a time (at your own comfort level) until you are ready to jump in and take back control of your life.

Obstacle 2: Believing that "alcoholism" just means you drink too much

There are many different forms of alcohol dependency. In some cases, a victim drinks every day all day, and in some cases an addict drinks in "binges". You might even be surprised to know that habitual drinking (the habit of drinking at certain times or occasions, including to celebrate or to mourn) is a form of alcohol dependency. Alcohol addiction, no matter what form it is, is not something cut out of stone. The symptoms of alcoholism vary from one individual to the next.

Overcoming this obstacle:

If you have considered quitting drinking, chances are you are suffering alcohol dependency. If alcohol has caused any problems in your life, and you are now conscious of the effects of alcohol in your life; then you are certainly ready to leap over this obstacle and recover from your dependency of alcohol.

Obstacle 3: Believing you can recover from alcoholism on your own

Many have tried and very, very few have been successful. If you really want to recover, you have to really face this fight against alcoholism realistically.

Overcoming this obstacle:

The hardest part is admitting to yourself that you are no longer in control. Whatever form your alcohol dependency has taken, alcohol has taken over. Admitting that you need help is not a sign of weakness; rather it is a great action of personal strength. More importantly, it is the most important action you can take towards recovering from alcohol addiction.

Beginning recovery from alcohol addiction

Your recovery from alcohol addiction begins at an alcohol treatment center. An alcohol rehab is your training base for the battle against alcohol dependency. Here you will find the many tools needed to fight off triggers.

Alcohol Detoxification

Cleansing the body of toxins is the kick start to moving on with your life. It is a lengthy, difficult, and often painful experience that can be nearly impossible to make it through alone. Alcohol detoxification at an alcohol rehab offers professional medical staff, 24/7, with the experience needed to help you through your withdrawal symptoms and back into a healthy body.

Counseling at an Alcohol Rehab Center

As mentioned previously, alcohol dependency takes on many forms. It is also not a matter of "drinking too much". Alcoholism is a disease, and often the symptom of another disease depression. Without qualified counseling at an alcohol treatment center, the underlying disorder is likely to continuously feed to a dependency on alcohol. The result? Continuously repeating the cycle of alcohol dependency.

An alcohol rehab counselor will treat both depression and alcoholism, so when you complete your alcohol rehab program you will be completely stronger and happier, inside out. More importantly, you will be ready for those triggers when they arise.

After an alcohol addiction treatment center

Just as your journey officially begins with alcohol detoxification, it is after you complete your program at an alcohol addiction treatment center that your journey continues. Armed with the tools to recognize triggers and fight urges, you will be back in control. The most important thing to understand that recovering from alcohol dependency is an action, and not just a simple process with a definitive ending.

Is Alcoholism Caused By Genetics or By the Environment?

Genetic and Environmental Factors

According to the National Institute on Alcohol Abuse and Alcoholism (NIAAA), a person's risk of developing alcoholism is 60% determined by his or her genetics and 40% caused by his or her environment. Assuming that these statistics are accurate, what can be done to reduce the chances of becoming addicted to alcohol?

Genetic Causes of Alcoholism

Regarding the genetic determinants of alcoholism, those who say, "nothing can be done" are not totally correct. True, a person cannot change his genetics. Knowing, however, that there is a history of alcoholism in a person's family, for example, can help a person "prevent" this potential problem from ever starting if he practices total abstinence. This kind of preventative thinking is an example of a "proactive" approach to problem solving.

More Proactive Problem Solving

The following illustration, however, is an even more extreme example of "proactive" problem solving that can affect the genetic basis of alcoholism. Maria, a young lady who drinks very infrequently, starts to date a young man named Kirk. As their relationship develops, Maria starts to notice that Kirk gets drunk on a regular basis. In fact, Kirk gets intoxicated at least two or three nights every week. What is especially problematic about Kirk's drinking is that he gets angry and combative when he drinks excessively. On numerous occasions, Maria has tried to encourage Kirk to seek professional help, but each time she starts to discuss his drinking, Kirk gets extremely defensive, starts yelling at her, and then goes to a bar to drink with his buddies. After a year of riding an emotional roller coaster, experiencing numerous hurtful arguments, and going through many difficult alcohol-related situations, Maria finally decides to break up with Kirk. What were the major factors for the breakup? Maria wants to have children and can't see having them with a violent and angry man who is so dependent on drinking alcohol. Moreover, Maria figured that since Kirk is exhibiting such irresponsible behavior in a dating relationship, he could possibly get even worse if they were to get married.

In this illustration, by breaking up with Kirk, Maria has stopped a negative cycle from going any further. Stated differently, by deciding to end her relationship with Kirk, Maria "prevented" the genetics part of the equation from ever becoming an issue.

Concerning Alcoholism, Age Matters

Another important alcohol-related statistic articulated by the NIAAA is that the earlier a person starts drinking alcohol, the more likely she will continue to drink her entire life. This being the case, it therefore makes sense to look for ways that will significantly reduce alcohol abuse by teens, preteens, and by young adults.

An Environmental Framework

Employing an "environmental" approach (as opposed to a genetics-based methodology), higher education seems to be a logical starting point for ways to reduce alcohol problems manifested by our youth. Indeed, since many teenagers go to college and because teen alcohol abuse IS a serious health risk, it is relevant to ask what college administrators can do to significantly reduce student alcohol abuse, especially when teenagers are some of the main "offenders." It is suggested that the following reactive and proactive measures help address this issue.

Reactive and Proactive Measures to Help Reduce Student Alcohol Abuse

• Establish immediate consequences for excessive drinking.

• Discipline repeat alcohol abuse offenders.

• Monitor the drinking activities in the sororities and fraternities.

• Notify parents about their children's drinking activities.

• Talk to the owners of local drinking establishments so that minors and/or intoxicated students are not served alcohol.

• Eliminate mixed messages about alcohol (for instance, removing alcohol advertisements from stadiums and from sports brochures).

• Inform and educate students about the long-term negative consequences of alcohol abuse.

• Increase the number of alcohol-free social and recreational activities that are attractive to students.

Generalizing the Results

With additional effort and some more thought, it seems reasonable to think that alcoholism experts and college administrators will be able to generate even more ways to effectively reduce alcohol abuse at institutions of higher education. Once this is accomplished, moreover, perhaps their findings can be adapted so that they will "work" in other institutions such as junior and senior high schools, boy scouts, girl scouts, churches, camps, and so on.

What is Alcohol Addiction? Alcohol Addiction Counseling and Treating Alcohol Addiction

The alcohol addiction counseling that is available today is much further advanced than the primitive approach used previously for treating alcohol addiction.

Alcohol addiction has existed for many years and is widely known as "alcoholism". Drinking, occasional overindulgence and getting a little 'merry' is nothing new, but most individuals do not take their drinking to the level of alcoholism. Those that do however, frequently see their lives falling apart and, all too often, find themselves in an early grave.

Until the establishment of Alcoholics Anonymous, a non-profit fellowship of recovering alcoholics trying to stay sober one day at a time, there was not much hope for those in the grips of severe alcoholism.

Most alcoholics were bundled off to mental institutions to go through delusion tremors (DTs) - a dangerous state which the body goes into during alcohol withdrawal - or forced into religion as a cure for their problem. Yet none of these 'cures' helped. As soon as the alcoholic would leave the institution or be alone, even for the shortest while, their return to drinking would be quick and imminent.

Chapter 3: Ways To Quit Alcohol

Is there an easy way toquit drinking? This question isquite hard to answer because everyone who has gone through alcohol addiction and recovered from it could share a thousand and one stories of difficulties and challenges during thequitting process. Sure, the ultimate solution to alcoholism is to stop drinking and be sober the rest of your life. However, just like many other things, this is much easier said than done.

Perhaps it is honest to say that there is no easy way to stop alcohol dependence. However, there may be some factors that can make the arduous process a little more bearable. These factors are often facilitated by treatment centers because they have proven to be helpful in many alcoholics' lives.

Peer Support

Meeting other people who are on the same boat can be very helpful in many ways. For one, they make you feel you are not alone. Sure, you may have family and friends who keep on telling you that you are not alone, but they are actually sober! They do not have any idea of how it's like to crave for alcohol as if it were your lifeline. Being with people who exactly know what you are going through can affect you more powerfully. They can inspire you as you can inspire them. You can help each other to get to the goal of steering clear from alcohol.

Help in Discovering Precious Life Lessons

Again, there is no easy way to quit drinking, but during the hard process, you will learn new precious lessons about life which you would not likely discover if you weren't in the fix. Peers, counselors, and therapists would help you realize many things about life and how much better it is to live it sober. A drunken life is a life of haze and chaos. Once you get the grasp of this truth, you will learn to appreciate the beauty of living independently from alcohol.

A Safe Environment

When you are surrounded by people who fully understand and support you, you will feel that your environment is safe and that you can make things happen in it. You will be protected from the temptation of alcohol and you will be able to move freely and more productively too. Without experiencing the mess of a drunken life though, you will not be able to recognize the value of this kind of environment.

All these factors could make the tough process of quitting drinking a lot more manageable. As withdrawing from the substance could even be fatal, everything that can teach you to be hopeful again would surely make a big difference. They will help you see things in a much better perspective, which will then encourage you to win the battle.

There is no easy way to quit drinking but there are ways to make it possible. If you have the willpower and you are surrounded by the right people, you can get over the problem and start living a much better life you and your loved ones deserve.

Alcohol addiction is destructive. Each alcoholic craves to quit drinking, just like they crave that next drink. Alcohol is an addiction that disrupts lives. Relationships with family, friends and work often suffer. There is no easy way to stop drinking. It requires commitment and will. There are steps that a drinker can take to stop drinking, and the time to stop is no better than today. With the right guidance and support, you can break the habit and cravings of alcohol.

First step to getting sober

Set goals. This is the first step. You must get rid of the negative thoughts such as "I can't do this", "I need that drink", "I can't stop the addiction" and so on. Get positive. You can do this and you will do it. You are in command and you have the control to pick up or put down the bottle.

Take a good look at yourself. Think about when you drink. When do you feel like you don't need a drink. Look at yourself. Take photos of yourself, record conversations, make notes. Get up and eat properly throughout the day. Record everything you eat and drink. Are you drinking alone, with friends, colleagues? Once you see your pattern, you can break it with a good strategy, a plan of attack.

Write down the benefits of not drinking. By writing the benefits, you will begin to boost your self-confidence and enhance your goal toquit drinking. Each drinking may have different reasons to quit. For some it may be health, for others it may be family, for others it may be for the good of themselves.

Create positive reminders for yourself. Write yourself positive notes, talk to yourself in a positive way and reinforce your road to victory.

Negative reminders are just as important. Here you think of all the disadvantages of drinking. Think of how depressing it is. Think of the negative factors it has in your life. The pain that it has caused you and your loved one. Repeat that you never want to go back to the bottle.

Change your companions. One of the hardest things that you may have to do is find a new set of buddies. It is definitely hard to be around alcohol when you are an alcoholic without drinking. Get a new set of friends that support your new lifestyle and break the cycle of drinking.

New routines: Remember that each day is the first day to the rest of your life. Now that you know that you are going to stop drinking you can wake up each day knowing you are fresh, announcing that you have given up drinking and that you are overcoming your addiction. You will need to make changes. It is time to take control of your lifestyle. Focus on diet, exercise and friends. Likely you have been neglecting all. Today is the day to start on your new lifestyle!

Stop Drinking Alcohol For Good

Alcoholism Is a serious problem In our society today. It ruins peoples lives and destroys relationships. People turn to alcohol as a way of dealing with the stresses and pressures of life, but the release is temporary and the consequences can be disastrous as well as costly.

Alcohol gives us a temporary release from our problems, but it has a detrimental effect on our health, relationships and our work environment. If you've got a drink problem you owe it to yourself, your friends and loved ones to stop this destructive habit.

Do you have a drink problem?

Do you get annoyed or irritated when people criticise your drinking?

Have you ever had a drink first thing in the morning to calm your nerves or to get over a hangover?

Do you sometimes consider cutting down the amount you are drinking?

Have you ever felt bad or guilty because of your drinking?

If you answered yes to any of the abovequestions then it is very likely that you have a drinking problem. If your drinking is destroying your relationships, job, health or getting you in trouble with the law, then you really do need to do something about it. Don't try to kid yourself that you can control your drinking, It never works and your addiction will win in the long run.

Imagine what a life without drinking could be like:

You will not be putting yourself or other people in danger

Your relationships will be better

You'll be healthier and live longer

You'll be happier

You'll look and feel better

You'll have more money at your disposal

You'll perform better in the workplace

You'll no longer make a fool of yourself

All of the above statements are true, can you see how great your life will become If you give up drinking?

But I can't imagine a life without alcohol?

I remember feeling that way too, I'd awake each morning and reach for the bottle. A day would never pass without me being under the influence of alcohol. I was unemployed, suffering from depression and suicidal and yet I still continued to drink. When you are drinking you don't think about anything else and such an attitude has a serious impact on your life.

There is a life without alcohol, a life where you can achieve your dreams and reach your full potential. I've not been drinking for two and a half years now and I've never had a relapse. I didn't have to rely on Alcoholics Anonymous, I stopped drinking all on my own, just as you can.

How to stop drinking

Think about the reasons why you drink and the occasions when you do.

Write down the bad experiences you've had as a result of your drinking

Work out how much you're drinking in a week

Make an appointment to see a medical professional to talk about stopping

Set a date to stop drinking

It doesn't look like you have to do very much does it? Your physician will be able to prescribe medication to get you through withdrawal process and it doesn't have to be unpleasant. I was a chronic alcoholic and I was dependent on alcohol to function on a daily basis and I was surprised at how easy it was to stop.

The problem is staying stopped, but the tools that I use make it easy. I'm not bothered by alcohol in the slightest. People can drink around me and I don't have a problem, indeed there is always alcohol In my house as my wife and son regularly drink.

Two and a half years ago I would have thought this was impossible and that I could never resist the temptation to drink!

Now I'm offering you the opportunity to do exactly the same, to defeat alcoholism and to live an addiction free life. I'll give you all of the tools and information to make your alcoholism a thing of the past. I want to help you to overcome your destructive habit and to lead a productive life where alcohol is no longer in control of you.

You'll gain the immediate respect of your friends, loved ones and work colleagues and to be able to achieve much more without alcohol.

You owe it to yourself, your family and your friends to overcome your alcoholism, so do something about it while you still can!

I used to wonder if I could ever quit alcohol, sometimes I just couldn't afford to drink and the thought of going without for a few days would instill me with panic. I would drink the cheapest, strongest and nastiest alcohol, so that gives you an idea about how desperate and financially dire my situation was! I was addicted for nearly thirty years, started the day with a drink and alcohol was never out of my system.

If you're serious aboutquitting, you could do it today, right after reading this article you really could make the decision to stop and never drink again.

Stopping drinking is easy, the hard part is getting motivated to do it.

How do you get to be motivated? It took me a long time to find the answer to thatquestion. The problem is when you are an alcoholic you put alcohol before

33

everything else, your family, friends and your health.

It doesn't matter how much damage your addiction causes, it's your best friend and confidante, remaining faithful to the grave. Could any other area of your life ever be so dependable?

How the hell can anything break such a strong relationship? You may well be aware of how much your habit is costing you financially, physically and emotionally...but you continue to drink, where is the logic in that? The reason you continue to drink is because your addiction has become a survival instinct.

The Method

* List the negative consequences of your addiction. The first step towards stopping drinking is to look at the damage your addiction is causing. Make a list of all of the negative things that have happened to you whilst drinking, the times when you

put yourself or others in danger, the blackouts, the times you embarrassed yourself, lost control of your bladder, hurt anyone else or did anything you regretted in the morning. If you are a problem drinker you'll most probably have a very long list. Do you really want to continue adding to the list? It's only a matter of time before you really do yourself or someone else some damage.

* Stop making excuses for you addiction. Accept the possibility that you can live without alcohol. If you really want to quit, you have to be honest with yourself, because whatever problems you have can be tackled effectively without alcohol.

* Seek medical advice. If you are physically dependent on alcohol,quitting can be dangerous and can result in death. Your Physician can provide you with advice and medication to help you to quit. You may also get the incentive to stop drinking when your Physician reveals what damage

alcohol has already done to you. He or she may also be able to arrange counseling for you and detoxification if necessary.

* Beware of Alcoholics Anonymous. Think carefully before going to Alcoholics Anonymous for help. Alcoholics Anonymous recovery statistics really aren't that great, their 12 step program is not flexible and will strip you of your own personal power and identity. There are better alternatives, Rational Recovery (in my opinion) is by far the best option available for the alcoholic.

* Develop an ongoing strategy and discover alternatives. Staying off alcohol really isn't that hard, since Iquit I've had to deal with the death of someone I loved dearly and drinking alcohol never even crossed my mind. I live in a house where I am the only person who does not drink (there's always alcohol in the house). Alcohol is always around me, but luckily so are non-alcoholic alternatives. Non

alcoholic beers are available in most bars and restaurants and there are plenty of non alcoholic drinks to choose from. On my Stag night I drank orange juice and watched with amusement as my friends got incredibly drunk and made fools of themselves whilst I managed to retain a sense of dignity. (It was a great feeling!)

* Try self hypnosis and meditation. You may find it useful to write some affirmations, affirmations will make it easier for you to deal with recovery. The biggest problem I had was with my self-confidence and self-esteem. I recommend reading "Feel the fear and do it anyway" by Susan Jeffers. I found this book was a lifesaver during the early stages of my recovery. I would also recommend that you look at cognitive behavioral therapy. I found CBT was an effective way of dealing with my core beliefs about myself and life.

* Give your life a purpose! If you've lived solely for alcohol, there is going to be a

large gap in your life and you may well experience all of the sensations you'd associate with the loss of a lover. I launched myself into work and made a considerable amount of money online. I also personally felt a desire to help other people overcome their addiction and that is why I set up Addictvoice, I also became drawn towards spirituality.

Quitting drinking is not going to be an easy ride but in doing so you will become a much stronger person. You'll become more confident and not reliant on alcohol every time you face a problem. You will never suffer from those terrible hangovers which make you unable to face work. You'll be in complete control of your faculties and will never embarrass yourself in public. Your close relationships will become stronger and you will get a great deal of respect from the people you love. You really do owe it to yourself to stop drinking, but you can only do so if you are prepared to change and to take responsibility for your life, and only you can do that.

Chapter 4: Understanding Alcohol

Alcohol is a legally produced substance that decreases stress and inhibitions; it includes a wide variety of partial effects, from poor coordination to slurred conversation. Not everyone who takes beverages is an alcoholic, but anyone whose life is adversely affected by alcohol is recognized as a liquor employ disorder. Consumption of alcohol is usually between a glass or two in some forms, including ale, wines, and hard liquor.

Beer craving and abuse

Beer is an alcoholic drink made from normal water, barley, hops, and yeast. Compared to wines or hard liquor, beers have the lowest alcohol content by quantity (ABV). Beer's ABV ranges from about 2 to 12 percent, with commonly consumed beers (Budweiser, Coors Light, Miller Lite, Corona, Busch, etc.) having a 4 to 6 percent alcohol content range.

Beer consumption games have become rampant in universities in the U.S; the rise of craft beer has even made beer consumption fashionable, with microbreweries and home brewers pushing the limits on new flavors and tastes introduced. One side-effect of the *ale revolution* is that beers may have high degrees of alcohol compared to the typical home craft - some are up to 11% or 12%.

Even individuals who drink during friendly activities or only drink craft beer are susceptible to an alcohol use disorder; meanwhile, it is true that "cultural drinkers" continue to drink while every other person has stopped.

Wine Dependency and Abuse

Wine is made out of fermented grapes or other fruits such as pomegranates or berries; mostly, it is sold as white or red with several taste profiles. Chardonnay, Pinot Grigio, Riesling, and Moscato are types of white wines while Merlot, Cabernet, Pinot noir, and Zinfandel are reds.

Types of Wine Produced from Grapes

Compared to beer, wines have an even more increased amount of alcohol; the common dose of wines (5oz) is relative to alcohol consumption content of 12oz of liquor. Wines tend to be taken at dinner parties or alongside cheese and crackers; its position as an "elegant" drink makes it difficult to recognize when someone becomes addicted to it.

Women constitute 59% of wines drinkers in the U.S and are mostly the target audience in ad campaigns promoting the drink. Women have less body mass and less water than men in their bodies; when consuming wines, the form diffuses the alcohol, meaning women have a high concentration of alcohol in their bloodstream than men. This makes women become quicker impaired and expose their brains and other organs to more alcoholic harm when they drink wine. Because of this, women are susceptible to alcohol disorder; however, both gender can develop a problem with wines.

If you or someone you love is addicted to wine, and takes it regularly or uses to evade stress or depression, addiction might be lurking around and you should get immediate help for any wine addiction.

Liquor drinking and Abuse

Liquor is the general term for hard drinks or spirits like tequila, vodka, gin, rum, and whiskey. Alcohol includes a higher ABV than ale or wine, which is often blended with sodas, juices, or water. The typical dose of liquor is 1.5 oz. Carbonation improves the absorption of alcoholic drinks into the bloodstream, so taking alcohol blended with soda could cause quicker intoxication. The reduced liquor content makes them better to consume, producing a higher risk of abuse and drunkenness. Many long-time drinkers associate different beverages with different feelings of intoxication; technology is yet to prove this, with studies showing that liquor has the same effect on everyone, regardless of the type of drink being consumed.

However, the setting where liquor is consumed may affect the drinker's belief of intoxication; someone having a glass of wine at dinner is more likely to experience exhaustion and happiness, while tequila at a high-energy party can create a much different sort of intoxication.

People who have severe alcoholic disorder may think they can't start their day without a swig of vodka or can't complete it without a cup of whiskey. Whatever the sort of liquor consumed, any kind of alcohol has the potential of being addictive.

Understanding Binge Drinking

A subset of binge drinkers are men who consume five or a higher level of alcohol or women who drink four or higher in two hours.

An infrequent binge drinker would probably quit on his or her drinks; someone who's an addict might want to finish all the drinks and might need support to get off the table; often, prolonged binge drinking can develop into alcoholism.

The Immediate after-effect of Alcohol

Alcoholic beverages are a central nervous system (CNS) depressant such that it decreases mental and bodily movements;

drinkers may experience a decrease in emotions of panic or stress. It is commonly touted as an energizer, meaning drinkers will feel self-confident in a gathering and less concerned about what others think about them.

Because alcohol consumption is legal and generally accepted in many cultures, it's hard knowing the difference between its free use and abuse. Generally, any use of alcoholic beverages leading to negative effects is recognized as abuse. Many of the negative effects of alcohol include:

physical harm or illness.

Strained relationships.

Problems at work.

Financial difficulty.

When abuse becomes more frequent, it could deteriorate into addiction.

Dependency on Alcohol

Alcoholic addiction, also known as alcoholism, means having a craving for alcoholic drinks as well as not being able to resist drinking, even though it causes extreme personal or sociable harm. Symptoms of alcoholism include frequently eating more than necessary, wanting to avoid drinking but struggling to, developing a tolerance for alcoholic consumption, having a relapse, allowing personal and professional commitments to suffer in support of drinks, and spending more time indulging in alcohol.

High-Functioning Alcoholics

There's a particular class of alcoholics referred to as high-functioning alcoholics. Individuals who are high-functioning alcoholics prevent their addiction from interfering with their professional and personal lives.

One New York article estimated that as much as half of all alcoholics are high-functioning alcoholics. Lawyers, professors, and doctors constitute a large part of the individuals. High-functioning alcoholics rarely recognize they are having problems until they face severe alcohol-related implications. The risk of high-functioning alcoholism is that it could continue for a long time without the addict ever realizing they are having issues.

Alcoholic beverages and other drugs

Since it is prevalent in today's culture, alcoholic drinks tend to be abused alongside other drugs. Just like a CNS depressant, alcohol poses a substantial risk when mixed with other drugs, such as benzodiazepines and several painkillers. Alcohol consumption alone could be dangerous, but merging it with various other chemicals can be lethal.

What is Alcohol Use Disorder?

Many people in the U.S end their day with a glass of beer or wine, and how do they know when they exceed their alcoholic limits? How do you know when you've crossed the alcohol consumption usage disorder (AUD)?

Drinking "in moderation" means having only 1 drink daily if you're a female and only two as a man. One drink equals:

1.5 ounces of liquor (like whiskey, rum, or tequila).

5 ounces of wine.

12 ounces of beer.

Another way to examine your drinking habits is to consider the average number of drinks you consume in a week.

For women, *"heavy"* or *"hazardous"* drinking means a lot more than seven drinks per week or more than three in a day; for men, it's a lot more than 14 drinks weekly, or more than four each day.

Alcoholic Use Disorder

Dangerous drinking could be the symptom of a condition called alcohol use disorder, it's a chronic disease that affects the brain. About 16 million people - adults and children -- in the U.S. have it. Sometimes your parents' genes can put you in danger, your physical and psychological environment can also put you in danger.

There are so many symptoms that can indicate that someone is suffering from AUD. Many of the symptoms include:

An uncontrollable urge to drink.

Inability to control how much you drink.

Negative thoughts when you're not drinking.

Drinking in risky situations.

Drinking that prevents responsibility.

Drinking even though it causes problems or makes them worse.

Neglecting activities that are essential due to alcohol.

You will see mild, moderate, and severe types of AUD, which depends on your symptoms. You're more likely to have AUD if any of the following happens.

You can't relax or fall asleep without drinking.

You need a drink to start your day.

You need to drink to become social.

Alcohol is a way to escape your feelings.

You drive after drinking.

You mix alcohol with other medications.

You drink while you're pregnant or nursing a child.

When your family asks how much you drink, you don't tell the truth.

You harm people or become angry when you drink.

You find it difficult to remember everything you did while drinking.

Your responsibilities suffer due to your drinking.

Drinking has caused you legal problems.

You've tried to avoid drinking but failed.

You can't consider quitting alcohol.

To feel the results of alcohol, you must drink more and more.

You experience symptoms such as shakiness, nausea, sleep issues, and seizures; once you've stopped drinking for a while. The more of these symptoms that manifest, the more serious your AUD can be.

Effects of AUD

Even if your case is mild, it could have a huge effect on your physical and mental health.

For some, AUD could cause:

Memory loss.

Hangovers.

Blackouts.

Long-term results include:

Stomach problems.

Heart problems.

Cancer.

Brain damage.

Long term memory loss.

Pancreatitis.

High blood pressure.

Cirrhosis, or scarring of the liver

You're also likely to be in danger that could increase your probability of being hurt or dying:

Car accidents.

Homicide.

Suicide.

Drowning

AUD affects those around you too; your drinking might damage your relationship with your family due to anger problems, assault, neglect, and abuse. Women who are pregnant risk a miscarriage. Their baby is likely to have fatal alcohol consumption syndrome and a high prospect of dying from SIDS.

Chapter 5: Morning Drinking

When it comes to the drinking problem, there are a few fairly nonsensical indicators—things like drinking alone and experiencing memory loss. I doubt there is a serious drinker on the planet who has not had drinking induced memory loss, to one degree or another, unless they are one of the temperate few who have never drunk more than they expected. As for drinking alone, certainly, anyone who has a glass or two in front of the telly one or two days a week has much less of a problem than someone who drinks to oblivion with friends (or acquaintances) in the local pub or bar every night.

Morning drinking is another one, often referred to as a symptom of drinking problems. However, that does not mean that someone who had a morning drink at a wedding, or at Christmas, or at the airport, had a drinking problem.

As you can see, all these so-called signs of drinking disorders are very subjective, but I agree that morning drinking, if not a symptom of having a drinking problem per se, can be a big step on the path to chronic alcoholism.

My "morning drinks" were the middle of the night drinks.

Whenever I drank, despite being completely shattered, I would still wake up at three or four in the morning, nervous and utterly 16

17

ALCOHOL EXPLAINED

So, if you take a morning drink just to get rid of the worst of the hangover, that may well be the case, but in no time at all, one drink will become two-then-three-then-four, and soon you'll just embark on another morning drinking session just to get started.

This is exactly what happened to me when my drinking at night went from one to two to three to four, and so on. The problem is that it doesn't only raise the number of drinks, but also the amount of time it takes to drink them. The rise is gradual (as our drinking does), and, as always, it's a sudden wake-up call that makes us realize how bad things are deteriorating. We've all got our low points or rock bottoms. You have some if you're anything like me, but one of my lowest points was waking up nervous, anxious, and unable to sleep at night, getting up and sitting on the couch and drinking away, and just when I felt sleepy enough to go back to sleep, hearing the morning alarm go off and then discovering that I was utterly stunningly drunk, so exhausted I could hardly keep my eyes open, and having a full day at work ahead of me.

Chapter 6: Five Stages To The Bottom

So, we have discussed a strategy. Unfortunately, as a rule, a "quit drinking" conversation starts from the end - with tactics. At the very beginning of the conversation with the doctor, patients and others literally throw themselves with questions: "What can you offer?", "What is it called?" "How much does it cost?" Important, very important questions, but they should be asked second. First, you need to understand what the patient wants to get. It is impossible to discuss what to go on if you have not decided yet where. At the same time, if there is a point on the map, you will get there. How? It does not matter! Though walking, whatever. The main thing - you know where. If a person really made a decision, then everything will become easier and clearer.

Five steps lead us to such decisions. This is denial, anger, bargaining, despondency, and reconciliation. These five stages are a universal algorithm for solving all problems that cannot be solved by willpower.

For example, we walk along the road and see an unfamiliar beast. The first thing we will experience is the denial: There is no problem, the beast is peaceful; it does not threaten us - just pay no attention. Most of the tasks we solve in this way - we do not pay attention.

But, if we see that the beast begins to threaten us, growls, behaves aggressively, we also begin to behave aggressively - we get angry, stamp our feet, raise a stone. Everyone reacts differently. Very often, going to the door, and trying to turn the handle, we pull it, if it does not immediately open. This method is also quite effective in most cases.

But, if this also did not help, then the intellect turns on, and we begin to bargain. In the case of the beast, we will offer him friendship, sausage, and try to distract him. We need a compromise or full benefit.

Having tried all the methods and have achieved nothing, we will begin to show the beast that we ourselves are afraid of it. Sometimes it works.

And only if this did not help, we will understand that we need to make a choice: either go and let them bite or change the methods.

It is important that reconciliation is not a solution, it is a choice, but a choice only between two paths. There will be no third. We tried to find the third, while we bargained, but did not find.

The same steps can be traced in the decision: "I am an alcoholic."

It all starts, as a rule, with denial. It seems to man, and to others that nothing terrible is happening. Events are perceived as strange but funny. Often relatives are even offended by the assumption of alcoholism by a family member. Patients themselves, as a rule, starting to explain their behavior, build phrases starting with the words "just ..." "I just went over it a bit" "It just happened." At this stage, people turn to numerous psychologists, psychotherapists, astrologers, and other specialists and non-specialists, with only one goal - to find a simple explanation of what is happening. Explanations are found - stresses, politics, stars, etc. A person can be in denial for quite some time.

In general, you need to understand that in alcoholism, the terms are long. This beast does not want to immediately kill the victim. Dates are not calculated in months, or even years. These are decades, lives, and generations.

Most often, denial lasts 10-15 years, then a person gets angry. In this state, the problem becomes apparent. This does not mean drunken anger, but what happens to a patient in a sober state. Coming out of another binge, such people begin to blame everyone for what is happening. They are determined to change the situation once and for all, but as a result, they see the "normal" use of alcohol. Under the "normal" refers to the use without consequences. There is no question of controlling the dose: "I will drink as much as I want!" The main thing is that without consequences. To understand that this will never happen, this person cannot say this to me, and therefore begins to look for the guilty.

Man is angry at himself. But anger cannot be accepted on oneself, and therefore it spreads to others. It's a shame that during this explosion, anger spills over to loved ones. The pattern is also obvious - whoever is closer got the most.

As a rule, a person does not stay in anger for long. Anger quickly tires, though. However, some like it. Such people can stay in it for several decades, fighting their shadow. Causing harm to themselves and others, they seek out everything bad in everyone seeing the enemy.

Sooner or later, a person begins to understand that there is some problem, but he is still not ready to make a decision. In this case, the third begins, and the most terrible phase is bargaining. This stage is really the worst, if only because it is the longest. Most alcoholics die, continuing to bargain, and failing to go further. Bargaining is what doctors most often see.

At this stage, patients determine their condition using lexical evasions: "I'm probably an alcoholic, but not yet chronic" or "I'm a household drunk."

The bargaining goes in everything, not only in definition. Consumption patterns are being built that are constantly changing (only three glasses, only in the evening, only on holidays). The schemes collapse like sandcastles, but, returning to their anger, the patient begins to bargain again for the next scheme. At the same time, intelligence works at breakneck speed, bringing only new losses.

I would like to tell you more about the losses. The fact is that during a bargain, a person can lose and often loses everything. Absolutely everything: money, health, love, faith, respect. This bargaining is meaningless since it is useless to bargain with a creature devoid of morality. Alcoholism is a creature from another world; there, in the underworld, there are no concepts of good or evil. Haggling with addiction is as stupid as reading sermons to mosquitoes about biting badly. The disease definitely decided to suck you to the last drop, and no arguments will convince her. An alcoholic plays infernal roulette, loses, but continues to bet. Helpful logic helps him lose everything: "If I lost 10 times, then I will definitely win in the 11th!"

On this path, a person has a dangerous feeling that he is still doing something. To the question: "How are you?" He replies: "So far, bad. Recently, there was binge again, but I'm working on the problem." He is sure that he lost the battle, but not the war. The knowledge that interests him relates either to the use of technologies (the so-called drinking culture), in which he is "helped" by the advertisement and the "experience" of friends. Or a search for excuses: why am I drinking wrong? Here, unfortunately, a huge "bear service" is provided by psychologists, astrologers, and other consultants who start a conversation with

the phrase "you are not an alcoholic ..."
How often do you see people using
intelligence to build an alcoholic alibi: "I
have eustress," "crisis like Martin Eden's,"
"the hard work that makes everyone
drink," not to list all. The science-like
nature of these explanations is striking.

But, nevertheless, alcoholism continues to
collect its terrible harvest. The patient will
give everything, even what he hid "for a
rainy day." He will give himself, having
come to this satanic temple, and
sacrificing all.

The worst thing is that spiritual values are
lost. That for which a person could stop
drinking. It is very typical that an alcoholic
tries to stop drinking for his family. When
he states this, he does not lie! He really
loves his wife, children. For a while, he was
in a dry pause; as a rule, this worked
wildly, feeling guilty. It seems that
everything worked out. But, after a few
months, when the will of the disease

prevails, the failure is repeated again. Trying to explain to himself what happened, the patient comes to the conclusion: "I have a bad family." For the sake of this family, he will never stop drinking.

No matter how many times he later creates a family, each time he will have to find flaws in it in order to drink.

If you stop drinking for work, it turns out that the profession is uninteresting. There will be nothing left; all life will be lived in vain. It turns out that the only way out is to get drunk.

In no case should you stop drinking for something else but you! Having to spoil the most valuable for excuses will be painful and incomprehensible. It has already been mentioned that such decisions are made only for themselves, for yourself, because you have come to such a conviction!

Trading daily for years, the patient begins to acquire the "stigma" of the craft. Just as a shoemaker can be recognized by the stoop, a teacher by voice, and a policeman by sight, and the trader has characteristic features.

Firstly, in trade, there is no faith. You can't take the proceeds in an envelope; you need to count. If they brought a box, let them open it. In the same way, an alcoholic never believes in 100 percent and never in anything. If he is shown to a person who has stopped drinking and has not been drinking for 5 years, the "merchant" will draw conclusions for himself: either he drinks, but imperceptibly, or did not drink at all, or will soon get drunk. It is hard to believe that there is treatment, help if you do not believe in the result.

Secondly, there is always a third way in trade. From the very beginning, trading was the art of compromise. If the merchant is not able to solve the problem, not as it should, but as it can, he will not receive benefits. Is it good or bad? It's good for a merchant, bad for an alcoholic - because his life is the subject of bargaining. And the "customer" is a creature more powerful than him. A creature that has already destroyed more than one billion people. But the search for the third way takes the patient's mind completely. Even in a conversation on this subject, it is very difficult for the patient to answer "Yes" or "No." Everything revolves around "probably," "maybe," "suppose," "what if suddenly ..."

Thirdly, the merchant firmly believes in a pagan miracle. Surely someday the necessary deal will turn up, I will behave correctly, and then the size of the gain will be such that I have enough for the rest of my life. But for this, you need to observe the rituals: "don't take money from your running capital," "say the right words," etc. If we are talking about the seller, this is just funny.

This phenomenon takes a completely different turn in alcoholics. These patients are absolutely sincerely convinced that there are "Naltrexone" pills "for binges" (not for alcoholism). They are constantly looking for some additives, herbs, sorcerers. Confidence that if you search "as it should" - you will find something that no one knows about takes on the form of super-valuable ideas.

By plunging into bargaining more and more, a person becomes confident that he has become a specialist. The most typical phrase: "Doctor, I don't need to tell anything. I know everything!" The naivety of judgment is not visible to the patient, since he really went a long way, very tired, but moved in a circle. So he didn't leave anywhere, he lost everything without finding anything. How can a person learn something new if he is sure that he knows everything?! In order to go on a journey, a traveler must assume that he has not been everywhere. In the same way, an alcoholic will be able to understand something only if he understands that he does not understand anything.

During bargaining, there are situations of temporary dryness. This is not sobriety, namely, dryness, because the decision is still far away. This is a situation when a person has already lost almost everything, but health is still left. There is nothing to take from him, but he can earn. And then alcoholism seemed to let him go. A person suddenly decides that he will not drink for a year or two, and does not drink. It works, and makes friends, a family appears. As a rule, everyone believes that he will never drink again. Although, in a conversation on this subject, the alcoholic himself suggests that sooner or later, he can still drink. Of course, not like before, but soon the vow will end. The word can and is the pitfall that this ship will crash about. He cannot help but drink. After all, the rope on the neck remained! And when you "walk up your sides," you will be pulled again, and you will have to come and leave everything again – another vicious circle!

Few manage to complete the bargain in life. Most patients die, continuing to bargain, but if all the same, the bargaining is over, the patient proceeds to the most unsightly situation - to despondency.

Being discouraged, the patient already agrees that he is an alcoholic; he does not argue, does not bargain, does not seek contradictions in words. He understands that he is drunk, but believes that this should be done carefully. There is no doubt that alcoholism turned out to be stronger, but it is reliable that at least he will be allowed to die without pain. A person is no longer looking for a good job, although, as a rule, he continues to work in order to drink. He is not trying to restore relations with loved ones; he even eschews them, realizing how bad it is. All judgments, intentions, fantasies are built, taking into account how he will drink at this time. Whether, after drinking, will be able to finish the job, or is it better not to start it. There is no doubt that he will drink. Such people are not aggressive, although others show concern for them, experiencing biological disgust. They reckon with a drunken bully and despise the homeless, although, from a person in gloom, the harm is much less. It would be logical to show compassion for him, but not understanding how this could happen, people feel fear. Fear that generates aggression.

Be that as it may, but despondency is a step forward.

Only after these circles of hell does a person come to reconciliation. To the situation of choosing from two possible options.

There are no barriers at these five stages. Easily out of gloom a person can go to bargain or even show anger. Angry about it, make sure of denial. As a rule, after all, bargaining is the most frequent manifestation, because, exactly, the soul rolls into it every time.

Those who are fortunate enough to make a choice in the direction of freedom are changing so much that it is rather worth talking about rebirth. Even if such a person has breakdowns, he no longer hides them but analyzes them. He is extremely interested in everything that can help him; he is trying to be crystal honest with himself. He wants, and sooner or later, he can be responsible for himself.

But making a choice is not easy. Bargaining instilled a desire to find the "third option," and therefore, the situation "go left - go right" does not suit. An alcoholic is looking for a "door in stone." He is confident that if you are a little trickier, you will still be able to deceive, slip through. Such people say: "Yes, alcoholism is a terrible evil. This is a plague that has already claimed many of my friends. This is grief. But I still try to go around the edge, not to fly off this turn, especially since I have really important reasons for drinking."

Paradoxically, the one who made the choice "I will drink, drink and die" has a better chance than the one who made no choice. It so happens that, having come to the conclusion: "a bottle is a ladder to heaven," a person is still horrified and changes his mind, but, pay attention, he already had at least some solution. It is much worse when a drowning man cannot grasp one edge of an ice hole. This means only one thing - he will continue to sink.

What is the "Bottom," and What is the Ultimate Way Out?

All who have received sobriety described the time when they experienced a sense of bottom. The bottom from which they managed to push off. There is such a feeling, but it's descriptions always look very strange. On the one hand, you need to feel it, but at the same time, they always warn: "Look, don't miss it! There is no bottom in the swamp!" People around are waiting for the bottom to come and ask: "What are the signs that a person has already reached a dead end?" There are no such signs. This feeling is mental; it is without sensations, without objective indicators.

When a person graduates from school, he is overwhelmed with a feeling: "This stage is over, now everything will be different!" But there were no sensations. There was no pain in the forearm, no temperature, no rash. What clinical analysis will show that a person decided to marry, become a poet, or go to another country?

It turns out that there is a sense of the bottom, but you won't run into the bottom with your heels. Rather head, or where a person's soul is? It is very difficult to determine: what is the bottom of an alcoholic and if he is already or not at the bottom.

How many times had to see patients who, due to frostbite, which happened while drunk, had to amputate their fingers. How many people committed terrible crimes while intoxicated. Sometimes an alcoholic even partially realizes that he is doing poorly and consciously goes for it, believing that "after this, I will definitely quit drinking." But, some time passes, and everything returns again. Although it happens that insignificant losses (loss of telephone, quarrel in the family, loss of work) suddenly cause a person to feel horror and an understanding of the bottom. Sometimes relatives tell each other about such cases and make the wrong conclusion: "He will drink until he crashes the car. I'd rather break it!" It doesn't mean at all that if someone stops drinking after a divorce, the other drunkards will do the same. There is simply no universal recommendation. Thousands of people lost cars, families.

One gets the impression that a person draws this line for himself. But, having drawn, it no longer erases.

The bottom is really a state of mind. And he understood, then changed his mind, again proved something and returned. But what's important is that the bottom is just a choice, not a decision. There are those who say so to themselves: "I have long reached the bottom. I was knocked from below, and I went on."

The feeling that I am already at the bottom is a feeling of complete emptiness, an understanding of absolute loss. In fact, this is a recognition of defeat, not a temporary failure, but complete impotence.

Realizing that he has reached the bottom, a person recognizes himself not as a beggar, but as a debtor. One patient described this condition as follows: "I had a family where they were afraid of me, there was work that they did not respect me, there were a house and some things, but they did not bring me joy or peace. It seemed to me that I had all this for rent; in fact, all this did not belong to me..."

Recognizing this, a person gets the opportunity to change something, at least he has a choice. But recognition is not easy. Pride does not allow us to let fears go. It seems that impotence cannot be recognized, we must fight on, and everyone says: "you must fight, you must hold on."

The bottom is a refusal to fight.

Paradoxical as it may sound, it is precisely the rejection of the struggle that allows a person to change direction. One alcoholic said that he had a feeling that he had been trying for a long time to open the door until he realized that it was opening inside. You just had to stop pushing it. In fact, the refusal of attempts to change something by his will saves the alcoholic.

Many, trying to help an alcoholic, try to bring him to the bottom, indicating to him his loss. This is quite logical, but we forget that we are faced with a paradoxical disease that distorts the psyche. It is extremely rare to convince a patient that he has "everything as bad." Patients, like in a frying pan, try to get out, build endless arguments and excuses, and then, often, tired of making excuses, suddenly say: "Well, since everything is so bad, therefore, nothing more needs to be done."

Talk about this irritates not only the patient but also the one who is trying to lead them. As a rule, these losses are joint: not only did the patient lose several years of his life, but his family members also suffered. Therefore, the conversation takes place on increased emotional tones and is very reminiscent of the accusation. As already mentioned, a person with alcoholism is "ready" for the charges. He begins to "explain everything" - others insist - excuses are becoming more and more elaborate and aggressive. This "walking in a circle," as a rule, ends with a banal scandal that does not lead to anything but unnecessary stress.

As practice shows, the patient himself must come to this concept. Until a person independently experiences a feeling of complete loss, there is no point in convincing him. Therefore, it is better if, during a conversation, others do not talk about their losses, but about him. No need to make assumptions "if you did not drink." You do not know what would have happened in reality if the alcoholic hadn't drunk, and you would be "caught" on this logical mistake - be prepared. Tell us what really happened. After all, a lot has already been lost. Speaking about yourself, describe not losses, but your state of mind. What did you experience when it all happened? This will help you understand yourself.

Do not demand the result immediately. It often happens that a person must think, remember what they were told, compare, evaluate. And, sometimes, it is possible to draw a conclusion.

Chapter 7: The Way To Quitting

Alcohol: Committing To Change

Quitting alcohol is never easy, especially if you have been a constant heavy drinker for a long time. Of course, you would be giving up something that has become an integral part of your life, and something that has occupied more time in your life than anything else. Remind yourself that alcoholism is something that never brings anyone good, and it is not something that you should continue in your life because of the harm it can bring not only to you and your physical health, but also to your family and friends.

It is understandable if you think that you cannot do it on your own, or that you do not know how you would be able to quit your addiction. Overcoming your addiction is not an easy task, and for many, it is a really difficult road to take. It definitely would not be easy, but if you are willing enough to give quitting alcohol and living a more fruitful and enjoyable life a chance, you will succeed no matter how difficult the path to quitting will be. Do not worry! Outlined below are simple steps that you could follow in order to help you stop drinking now!

Commit yourself to change. Deciding to quit drinking is not something that you simply realize overnight, and it does not come out of the blue. Thoughts of quitting may be something that you may have been considering for a significant amount of time, although you have done nothing about it at first. When you decide to quit, it is important that you completely think it through, affirm to yourself that you would be honest, and actually push through with quitting alcoholism.

The first step that you need to take in your journey towards quitting is actually accepting that you are, without a doubt, addicted to alcohol. It is, of course, normal to exhibit denial behaviors when faced with the thought of being addicted, but if you are to quit, you need to realize that you have a problem and that you cannot get out of it unless you acknowledge it. Still, even if you acknowledge the fact that you are addicted, you may still find reasons to stick with your addiction by making up excuses. When you feel that you need to think twice about it, rethink of how much your addiction is costing you financially but not only also with regard to how much time you spend with your spouse and how many things you can accomplish when you are sober.

Afterwards, create a list of pros and cons of being addicted to alcohol, or of drinking in general. In order to perfectly justify your reasons for quitting, make a table divided into two, with one side being labelled "benefits of drinking" and the other "benefits of not drinking". In the "benefits of drinking" side, list down all the benefits that alcoholism has brought you. Mostly, people write things in this area such as "drinking helps me to forget about all my problems in life", "drinking gives me pleasure; it is fun!", or "drinking has helped me ease my stress after long days at work."

On the other hand, on the "benefits of not drinking" area, write everything that you could do in life without alcohol. Remember that when you are sober, you could do a lot of things with a conscious mind and with sound judgment.

Firstly, you can put in this part of the table that your relationship with friends and your family will definitely improve. Committing time to being sober greatly helps in improving your relationships with your spouse and your children, giving you the opportunity to show affection and to make up for the time you have lost in drinking.

In addition, quitting drinking can also help in improving your health. Physically, with your body not having to always cope with high levels of alcohol, the body can begin repairing parts that have been severely affected by addiction such as your heart, muscles, liver, pancreas, and your digestive tract. Not only will it help your physical health, but it will also help your mental awareness as well. Quitting alcohol will allow your brain to recover, especially the frontal lobe which is the part that is most affected by alcohol. Being sober also gives you more time to do the things in life that you have not had the time to do when you were in the midst of being addicted.

Make clear goals for yourself. When you have decided to change, your next step would be to establish precise and very clear goals for drinking. Remember that when you decide on your goals, you have to be very realistic about it, specific in what you want to achieve, and clear with what you want to aim for. For instance, you can write on a piece of paper "I will stop consuming alcohol starting on this date: _____".

When are you going to start being permanently sober? Is it going to be within a week, a month, or within the next six months? Of course, you cannot just give up drinking all of a sudden – you will face withdrawal symptoms if you do this – so you have to think of ways as to how you would eventually come to a point where you will stop drinking entirely. If you wish to simply reduce your intake of alcohol, you need to think of which days you will be consuming alcohol, and how much alcohol you will allow yourself to take on those days that you can drink. If your ultimate goal is to completely stop drinking, limit your time of consuming alcohol to a maximum of two days a week.

When you have set your quitting date, you need now to carefully plan how you are going to help yourself achieve your aim. Here are some things that you must consider:

a.Getting rid of your temptations. If you are to quit drinking, you have to remove anything that could remind you of alcohol from your life. If you have alcoholic beverages lingering around your home, get rid of them. Remove everything that has to do with alcohol from your home, and in your office.

b.Tell your peers that you will be quitting. Tell everyone about your plan to quit. This will not only give them the chance to support you, but it will also give them an awareness of what you are planning to do so that they could avoid tempting you to go back to your old ways. If your friends are drinkers, ask them not to drink when you are with them.

c. Be sincere with the limits you have set for yourself. Respect the new rules you have put forth. When you have decided that you will not drink at home, respect that and do not bring any drinks to your house. In addition, accept the fact that you would not be able to go to social functions that have alcoholic beverages.

d. Move away from bad influences. There are going to be people who will not support you in your attempts to quit drinking. They might even make you reconsider your decision by telling you about how much fun drinking is, or how much it could help in forgetting problems. These people might even tease or mock your attempts to quit drinking. You do not need these people bothering you, so simply remove yourself from their presence. Avoid hanging out with them or entertaining what they say about your quitting. Just remember the things that motivated you to quit in the first place and the health benefits you can get when you succeed.

If this is not your first attempt at quitting, look back at your previous attempts and analyze what you should and should not do. There may have been reasons why you were not able to successfully quit in the past. Learn from the mistakes you made before and improve on them in this next attempt at quitting drinking. Try to recall the things that worked for you in your previous attempts, as well as those that did not work at all.

Chapter 8: Negative Effects Of

Underage Drinking

Reasons for Underage Drinking

There is no one reason for underage drinking, so in this section, let us briefly explore the most common reasons.

A common reason for underage drinking is that the adults around them are consuming a variety of substances. If they see others around them drink, smoke, or use other substances, their chances of trying the same increase. Also, young adults like the idea of experimenting. Another reason is that they see their friends smoke or drink. When their peers urge them to drink, the chances of indulging such requests are high. As clichéd as it sounds, teenagers believe that drinking alcohol is a normal part of the teenage experience.

When the media start popularizing the drinking culture, young adults start believing that it is okay to drink. When they see their favorite singers, actors, or any other characters on a show drink or smoke, they start thinking they should also try all this. When young adults are unhappy or if they cannot find a healthy outlet for all their negative emotions, they might turn to alcohol. Depending on the substance they use, they might experience feelings of bliss, energy, and confidence. The teenage years are seldom easy, and the experience of growing up itself can take a toll on a teenager's wellbeing. There have been numerous instances when teenagers start abusing prescription medicine for regulating their lives or managing stress. At times, they abuse prescription stimulants that give some additional energy required to improve their ability to focus and study. Likewise, they also start depending on alcohol because it gives them an outlet out of their frustrating lives.

Alcohol helps let go of any inhibitions. If a teen is rather reserved and shy, then he might believe that drinking alcohol will make him more confident. Alcohol alters the way an individual perceives reality and makes decisions. When a little bit of this rationalism goes out the window, it becomes easier to let go of any suppressed impulses.

Another common reason for underage drinking is boredom. An empty mind is the devil's workshop. Teenagers who hate the idea of being alone have trouble keeping themselves occupied or start craving for excitement. The prime candidate for this excitement is alcohol. Further, alcohol starts providing a common ground for interacting with other like-minded young adults and gives them a social outlet.

Instant gratification is quite tempting for anyone and not just teenagers. However, the ability of young adults to carefully analyze the repercussions of their actions is much less than adults. So, their developing minds often give in to the urge of instant gratification. Alcohol is a great source of instant gratification that teens desire. They not only know the effect alcohol produces but also know they can instantly derive their desired results. For instance, if a teen knows that he will feel better after a couple of drinks, then his sole motivation to drink is to feel better.

The teenage years and rebellion go hand in hand. During adolescence, children are stuck between overcoming their child-like ways and developing a more adult and matured persona. In this period of transition, they commit various acts of rebellion to try to understand their boundaries. Drinking alcohol becomes their go-to act of rebellion.

Harmful Effects of Underage Drinking

A young person's body is still growing, and indulging in underage drinking can effectively harm this development. Underage drinking also makes young people especially vulnerable to the long-term physical and mental harm caused by alcohol consumption.

Underage drinking, especially excessive and frequent drinking, is associated with a variety of negative consequences. The negative consequences of alcohol consumption can be an acute and immediate result of a single episode of excessive drinking that led to impaired functioning. It can result in fatal injuries or accidental deaths. Or the consequences of alcohol consumption can be accumulated and quite diverse, resulting in poor performance at school, broken relationships, and addiction. According to research, it is believed that about 70% of all drinkers who engage in excessive drinking are at a greater risk of making poor decisions with long-term ramifications by the time they reach the ages of 19 and 20. However, underage drinkers don't have to drink excessively to increase the risk of negative consequences. The risk of crashes associated with driving under the influence is higher in young adults than in adults, according to some studies. So, young adults and adolescents don't necessarily have to drink heavily to increase their risk of experiencing negative consequences.

Research also suggests that all those who indulge in underage drinking are at a greater risk of experiencing a variety of health problems, including insomnia, headaches, and unhealthy weight loss.

Usually, people don't take their first experience with alcohol seriously. It is not surprising that about 3 in every 10 young people who drink alcohol experience a negative consequence caused by their drinking. In this section, let us look at all the different risks associated with underage drinking.

Alcohol Poisoning

Excessive drinking within a short period can result in alcohol poisoning. In alcohol poisoning, the level of alcohol is so high that it has a negative consequence on different parts of the brain that regulate balance and speech. It also harms the nerves responsible for regulating your breathing and heartbeat. It also drastically reduces body temperature, leading to hypothermia. Alcohol poisoning can also cancel the gag reflexes, which increases the risk of choking to death, especially while vomiting. Over 4,000 hospital admissions for underage drinking because of alcohol poisoning were reported in 2014.

Injuries

Consumption of alcohol not only reduces your mental and physical abilities, but it also seriously impairs your judgment and body coordination. This stands true not just in adults, but also in adolescent drinkers. A combination of all these factors can cause accidents and even result in injuries. Your body weight and its ability to metabolize alcohol also dictate your state of inebriation. Since the body weight and body metabolism of alcohol are quite low in young adults, it leads to rapid and acute intoxication. Some research suggests that all students who tested positive for alcohol consumption were at a greater risk of getting injured or getting into accidents when compared to nondrinkers.

Acute Impairment

Alcohol impairs one's ability to make good decisions. Due to this, underage drinkers are at a greater risk of engaging in risk-taking behaviors that result in injury, illnesses, or in extreme cases, death. The acute consequences of excessive and frequent drinking might result in unintentional injuries and even death associated with driving or engaging in any risky behaviors after drinking. The most common risky behaviors after drinking include violence, homicide, sexual assault, suicide attempts, extremely risky sexual behavior, and vandalism. In a series of studies, it was observed that individuals who started drinking before the age of 15 were 12 times more likely to sustain unintentional injuries while under the influence of alcohol when compared to those who waited until 21 to start drinking. The same studies also suggested that underage drinkers are 7 and 10 times more likely to be involved in a motor vehicle crash and physical fight, respectively, after drinking.

Driving Under the Influence

The consequences of driving under the influence have received plenty of media attention and targeted policymaking in recent years. Several laws have been implemented to reduce the permissible blood-alcohol content (BAC) levels for underage drivers to almost zero or 0.02 at the most. There has been a substantial reduction in underage motor vehicles for fatalities related to alcohol consumption, but it is still a considerable figure. According to the data procured from the National Highway Traffic Safety Administration, it is suggested that about 69% of young adults who died in alcohol-related traffic accidents involved underage drinking in 2,000. Driving under the influence is not only a serious issue for underage drivers, but also for all their innocent victims. Though only 7% of licensed drivers in the year 2,000 were between the ages of 15 to 20, they accounted for 13% of all drivers involved in fatal motor vehicle accidents caused due to drunken driving.

Therefore, it is safe to say that the chances of underage drivers getting involved in crashes are quite high when they are drinking when compared to those who weren't drinking while driving. It is not just about driving under the influence but also the decisions they make associated with their safety start dwindling once drunk. For instance, according to a study, it was suggested that young adults are less likely to wear a seat belt while in a car and are more likely to get in a car even if the driver is intoxicated. Unfortunately, around 40% of frequent heavy drinkers admitted that they got into vehicles with an intoxicated driver.

Brain Development

The brain is still in its developing stage during the childhood and teenage years. Excessive consumption of alcohol negatively affects one's memory, the ability to react, learn and stay focused. All these factors are incredibly important during the school years. So, indulging in excessive alcohol intake during these years harms one's education. Research suggests that children who start drinking alcohol by the age of 13 are at a greater risk of getting poor grades, skipping school, and expulsion from school.

Excessive and frequent use of alcohol hurts the physical development of the brain structure, according to new research. The growth of the brain during infancy and childhood essentially concentrates on creating new brain cells with as many connections to the other brain cells as possible. During the teenage years, this developmental focus shifts from producing more neurons to creating efficient and effective neural pathways. There are two ways in which this creation takes place.

The first way is how the structure of a neuron is changed because of the myelin sheath around it. The myelin sheath helps with the speedier movement of electrical impulses within the brain. It essentially means that the ability of an adult to relay information from one part of the brain to another is quite high when compared to children. During adolescence, this process is concentrated in the prefrontal and frontal lobes. These are two parts of the brain responsible for various important aspects, such as organization, planning, and stalling an impulse.

The second change associated with brain development is related to synaptic refinement. Synaptic refinement is the process through which the connection between brain cells becomes fine-tuned so that only the efficient pathways remain, while the unnecessary ones are removed. As with the formation of the myelin sheath, even this process increases the speed and efficiency of transmitting and relaying information from one part of the brain to another. It, in turn, improves your overall reaction time. During the early teenage years, various developments start taking place in areas of the brain responsible for critically considering the consequences of actions and the ability to manage stress effectively.

In an animal study, it was noticed that alcohol consumption during adolescence has detrimental effects on both these processes of brain development. In this study, rats were given excessive and frequent doses of alcohol to mimic the alcohol use pattern of an adolescent heavy drinker.

Mental Health

One of the most common reasons why underage drinking occurs is that young people use alcohol as a coping mechanism. They believe that it helps cheer them up while reducing any worry about their problems. So, excessive consumption of alcohol over a period can result in a variety of mental health problems. In fact, there is evidence that suggests there is a close relationship between mental problems and alcohol misuse.

Substance Use and Abuse

Excessive drinking in an underage adult is a problem in its own right, but it is also directly related to engaging in other harmful behaviors, such as the intake of illicit drugs. When compared to nondrinkers, the chances of underage drinkers using tobacco, cannabis, or any other hard drugs are quite high, according to some research.

Unintentional Injuries

Alcohol not only leads to impairment in judgment and poor decision-making, but it also reduces body coordination. It is one of the reasons why alcohol is the leading cause of unintentional injuries. A significant portion of unintentional injuries and deaths due to dangerous and risky behavior other than driving is also related to alcohol consumption. In a study conducted in 1999, it was noticed that about 40% of underage victims and accidents, such as burns, drowning, and falls, all tested positive for elevated levels of alcohol. It is not just traffic accidents or unintentional injuries, but alcohol is also implicated in injuries and deaths associated with suicidal behavior and violence too. Excessive and frequent alcohol consumption is associated with an increase in negative feelings, such as hopelessness, suicidal thoughts, and suicide attempts.

According to the statistics released by the Centers for Disease Control and Prevention in 2001, it was noticed that alcohol was the leading cause in 36% of homicides, 8% and 12% in female and male suicides, respectively, in the under 21 age group. According to a report published in 1994 by the National Centre on Addiction and Substance Abuse, it was noted that about 95% of all violent crimes and 90% of college rapes committed on college campuses involved the use of alcohol by the victim, the assailant, or both parties.

Sexual Activity

Another set of common alcohol-related problem is sexual violence, unplanned sexual activity, or even unprotected sexual activity. In a publication titled "A Call to Action: Changing the Culture of Drinking at U.S. Colleges," it was reported that over 70,000 students between the age groups of 18 to 24 years were victims of alcohol-related date rape or sexual assault. Some studies also suggest that sexual assault, assault, and date rape on college campuses show alcohol as one of the factors impairing the behavior of assailants and victims alike.

It is not just the vulnerability of experiencing or committing sexual assault; young people who drink more also are at a greater risk of engaging in risky sexual behavior and activities. According to a study, it was noted that around 44% of sexually active teenagers reported they are more likley to engage in sexual intercourse if they were drinking. Alcohol leads to judgment impairment, and therefore, the chances of making any rational decisions while drunk are quite low. So, someone who might have normally not engaged in risky sexual behavior is more likely to engage in such behavior while under the influence of alcohol.

Alcohol also reduces inhibitions, and it is one of the leading causes of risky behavior. Young people choose to drink even when they thoroughly realize that alcohol impairs their decision-making and prompts them to engage in sexual behavior that they normally wouldn't if they were sober. According to a college survey conducted by the Boston University School of Public Health, it was shown that those who had their first drink before they were 13 years old are twice as likely to engage in unplanned sex and twice as likely to engage in unprotected sexual activities.

Property Damage

Another set of consequences associated with behavior and activities under the influence of alcohol include vandalism and property damage. According to a report, it is believed that the chances of intoxicated youths committing these acts, regardless of the age, is quite high, especially on college campuses, when compared to their sober counterparts.

Long-Term Effects

The long-term effects of a single decision made under the influence of alcohol are undeniable. Some of the immediate consequences of it might be death or injury, but all these consequences have long-term repercussions too. Also, excessive consumption of alcohol at a young age implicates the long-term changes in a youth's prospects in the future. All those individuals who start drinking before the age of 15 years are at a greater risk of dealing with lifelong problems. For instance, individuals who start drinking before the age of 15 are at a greater risk of developing alcohol dependence later in their life. Also, the chances of developing alcohol dependence in the future are about 40% in such youths, while it is only 10% in those who start drinking after they reach the legal drinking age, according to a study.

Excessive and frequent use of alcohol is also associated with depression, low self-esteem, antisocial behavior, dependency on other substances, and anxiety. In a report, it was noted that around 25% of college students who were performing poorly in college were frequent drinkers. Underage drinkers are, therefore, at a greater risk of developing the different health problems discussed in the previous chapter.

Chapter 9: Change The Way You

Drink

After the person has changed the way he or she lives, it is time to change the way he or she drinks. This is very important, since the act itself has to be changed if the person really wants to prevent the abuse of alcohol, especially since he or she cannot assure that never again would he or she be able to drink liquor in the future. They have to know or to learn the right way of drinking liquor, to make sure that they have control over themselves whenever they drink liquor. Time will come when they will finally sit in front of a bottle of alcohol and ask themselves how in the world they should carry themselves. If they still have not learned how to rightfully drink alcohol, then the old ways will come again, and the abuse and addiction will again enter into their system, creating again the old problems that once they thought were already a thing of the past.

It has been well accepted that something that is a part of a person's past cannot be erased totally in one sweep. Instead, that thing should be eradicated from his or her life one step at a time. If this is about alcohol addiction, and the person usually takes alcohol for, let's say, twice a week, then the first step is to take it for only once a week for one month. After taking it once a week for one month, it is high time to take it every 10 days three times a month. After taking it every 10 days for a month, then it is high time to take it only twice a month every two weeks. After taking it only twice a month, then it is high time they should take it for only once a month... and then decrease the intake again and again until they would experience alcohol intake for, let's say, every two or three months. In time, that person will realize that he/she has not been taking alcohol for half a year, since he/she did it step by step, without thinking too much of his/her mission. In all these, it is evident that when trying to overcome alcohol addiction, the method is not to erase it once and for all, but to lessen the intake little by little, until such time when the alcohol intake transpires for only once or twice a year. In other words, people should know how to drink the right way—not to totally prevent him/her from drinking, but to drink liquor in the right manner.

On the other hand, when trying to overcome alcohol abuse, then they should try lessening their intake of alcohol little by little. If, for example, the person normally drinks eight bottles of alcohol in one drinking session, then the first step would be to decrease the number of bottles to six bottles, for example. The second step would be to decrease it again to four bottles of alcohol. The third step would be to decrease it again to three bottles, until the time comes whey they only have to drink two bottles of alcohol in one drinking session. In the same way, the answer is not to totally eradicate the intake of alcohol, but to lessen the intake little by little, one step at a time. Think of it little by little to prevent being too overwhelmed by the mission of lessening the intake of alcohol.

Meanwhile, it is likewise important that a person trying to overcome alcohol abuse and addiction should be able to identify the danger zones of when and where they are most likely to drink alcohol. These danger zones they should prevent by doing other things or going to other places, instead of being around those danger zones on those most dangerous times of the day. Say, for example, the danger zone is at 7 pm after the day is over and work has already been settled, then it would be better to do breathing exercises during that time of the day—something that will keep them from feeling the effect of not taking in liquor during that time of the day. They can also try doing some yoga or some relaxation activities right within the room.

Meanwhile, if the danger zone is at the house of a friend that they tend to pass by when going home from work, then it is high time to use another road when going home from work. As the experts have said, getting over the moments of impulse two or three times will eventually lead to a zero impulse, until there is no need to take in anything. People do not have to be strong the whole day through. They only need to know their strengths and weaknesses, and the time and place when they are most likely to be pressured and prompted to take again some alcohol. They have to know their danger zones so that they will be ready to face them with the right tactics—something that is incompatible with the addiction, as

117

something that is difficult to overcome, such as alcohol, should be fought over. This means that people should be ready to face them square by square, especially during the most difficult time of the day when they feel instigated to again go back to their ritual of drinking alcohol. Once or twice, they may need to give themselves some break, but this should only take place when there is really nothing that can be done—nothing to stop the cravings for a little taste of liquor.

Chapter 10: Why Is It So Hard To Quit Drinking?

When faced with a drinking problem, the first thing that most victims will want to do is to search for successful ways of quitting drinking. However, the truth of the matter is that, these tips never talk about why is it so hard to quit drinking in the first place. Perhaps the best way of cutting down on alcohol is by understanding the root cause of the problem. Sure, you will come across many guides arguing that you should start by setting drinking goals, drinking slowly, watching out for peer pressure or asking for support. Arguably, this doesn't address the main problem at hand. So, this chapter will help outline some of the reasons why it's usually a big challenge to quit.

Letting Go of Your Best Friend

119

There are several common experiences that anyone who has been through alcoholism will bear witness. Right from the first time you drank alcohol, you knew that you had found a friend. For shy individuals, alcohol can offer them the confidence that they need to fit in to new social circles. The more you drink, the more alcohol will introduce you to new people. In a way, it acts as the confident friend who is always there to ensure that you are having fun. It will help you get over your dating shyness. For a while, you will gain the popularity you have always dreamt of. You will not be lonely as you once were.

From afar, alcohol is a problem solver. The self-esteem that you once struggled to deal with will be boosted in one way or another. After all, you are popular among your friends. This is what most people crave. Knowing that alcohol can gift you with this opportunity at the cost of just drinking is what keeps most victims glued to their bottles.

Unfortunately, the friendship that you create with alcohol doesn't last long. Yes, you might have depended on alcohol for varying situations, but in the end you will realize that you can't do without it. You will try hanging out with friends when you are not sober and the experience will be unbearable. Certainly, you will be bored to death and the next thing you notice is that you will be asking for a glass just to get you out of your sober mind.

So, why is it difficult to quit? One of the main reasons why you will find it difficult to quit is because you will be letting go of your best friend. This is a friend who seemed to always help you out of many situations, the problem solver, a shoulder to lean on and you can be sure that it will tuck you in at night.

The fear of letting go is what makes most people hesitant about quitting drinking. We are faced with the dilemma of not knowing what will happen after we cut off drinking. Frankly, we are never certain whether we can maintain the social circles we once had. Everything about the world of staying sober is what remains unknown. Arguably, this makes people hesitant to change for the better.

Admitting the Problem Exists

Another reason why addicts find it difficult to quit is because of their failure to admit that there is a problem. This is what is termed as living in denial. A victim will often be defensive about their drinking habit. It will not be surprising for them to argue that they can stop the behavior if they want to. This is a common excuse that they will give to their family and friends.

Others will be well aware of the alcohol disorder, but will be afraid to let go. In this case, an individual might have tried to quit previously but failed. The aftermath effects that they experienced are what make them hesitant to walk in that direction.

Alteration of Brain Chemistry

Individuals who have tried to quit drinking but have failed will always blame themselves. Most of them end up thinking that they are failures because they find it impossible to quit without asking for help. One thing that you should realize is that cutting off alcohol is more than just the willpower to do so. It goes far beyond your determination to stop drinking. Simply put, your brain has been hijacked. The good news is that you can regain control and change your life.

Alcohol dependence has numerous complex components which interact with the brain in complicated ways. The experiences that people go through and their journey to addiction varies. Nevertheless, the aftermath conditions are the same. Drinking alcohol occasionally gives one a relaxing and pleasant mood. People who choose to engage in infrequent drinking experience temporary changes in their brains.

On the contrary, consuming alcohol regularly and in large quantities affects the brain chemistry in profound ways. This makes it a daunting task to control your drinking patterns. With time, you develop a vicious cycle where you feel as though you need to consume more alcohol to experience similar effects. This drives you to increase the quantity of alcohol you consume and the frequency of your consumption. As such, the effect is that the alcohol will alter how your brain functions. Ultimately, this also changes how you feel.

Now, a prolonged use of alcohol will continue to change your brain chemistry. Eventually, your brain can no longer work as it used to. This leaves you in a situation where you need to ingest alcohol in order for you to feel normal. Think of it this way, the desire to drink alcohol is just like when you are hungry. The more you try to postpone your eating, the more you are affected by the hunger pangs. It's not easy to ignore these pains.

Therefore, you shouldn't beat yourself up that you have failed in your efforts to try and quit drinking. The important thing to realize is that, your brain has been affected in a huge way. Your call for assistance is what will make a difference toward your recovery.

Fear of Recovery

There's always a negative perception towards rehabilitation. It creates fear among those who are addicts. As such, this stands as another reason why victims are afraid to take necessary steps to ensure that they recover. The notion that there are unpleasant withdrawal symptoms you can go through can also scare one away from trying to quit alcohol.

The reality is that, indeed, it is not easy to quit drinking if you are already an addict. However, you ought to have it in mind that it is possible. There are a wide array of treatment centers where you can seek medical assistance. Individuals here are experts and they understand how best to help you detox. The best part is that there are medications which are offered to assist you in dealing with the withdrawal symptoms.

Looking at the bright side, you have to understand that there is nothing bad that can happen. Yes, you will go through several instances of unpleasant experiences, but after that you will have the chance to live your life again. You will have freed your mind from the cage that drinking created to hold you hostage.

Sure, there is no denying the fact that overdependence on alcohol creates a habit which is difficult to turn away from. Letting go is the hardest decision that you could ever make considering the fact that you will be saying goodbye to a friend you have known for years. Also, bearing in mind that you will be battling to regain control of your mind, it means that you will have to commit yourself to the process. If you are looking to get sober, the time to make a decision is now. Don't harm your body any longer. Take a stand and find the help you need.

Chapter 11: Dealing With The Effects

Of Alcohol Withdrawal

As has been underscored in the preceding chapter, overcoming your alcohol addiction necessarily entails your withdrawal from the use and abuse of any ingestible substance with alcoholic content. However, doing so will likely come with unpleasant consequences. Depriving yourself of alcohol after your body has become used to it will result in a condition called withdrawal syndrome.

Withdrawal syndrome comes about as a result of the sudden deprivation of alcohol in your blood stream. It is characterized by a number of physical symptoms. Note that this is the stage where your mind and body crave for alcohol the most -- certainly a major challenge on your journey toward full recovery.

Some of the symptoms of withdrawal syndrome include:

1. A general feeling of discomfort. Patients are not sure of what or how they are supposed to feel. What they do know is that they are restless and are saddled with a feeling of discomfort.

2. Cold sweats.

3. Nausea.

4. Foul body odor. As your body goes through the process of detoxification, you may notice that you are emitting a particularly odorous scent.

5. Vomiting.

6. Increased heart rate or palpitations.

7. Fever.

8. Irritability.

9. Volatile emotional state. The feeling of discomfort can result in an inability to maintain emotional control.

10. Bowel movement problems.

11. Nightmares. Apart from hallucinations, you may also experience awful nightmares more frequently than usual.

12. Trouble sleeping.

There are varying degrees of withdrawal syndrome based on your degree of dependence on alcohol. Most cases are actually tolerable. You will likely experience the symptoms for a week or two, possibly a month, after which the symptoms will go away on their own.

Withdrawal syndrome is not something that can be ignored. It is a very important part of the treatment process -- the final hurdle before you can finally claim your life back.

Keep in mind that extreme cases of withdrawal syndrome need medical intervention. There are clinics available especially for these kinds of cases. In incidents like these, patients are administered with various forms of medication to help the body relax and mitigate the general feeling of discomfort. It is highly recommended that you consult with your doctor prior to detoxification. If your withdrawal symptoms become unbearable or do not go away over time, definitely do pay a visit to your doctor and get help.

Chapter 12: Triggers

Sometimes when we are in a certain situation, place or with some people we will find a craving to have a small drink. Usually this is just a short period of time and controllable. Knowing how to react to these cravings and recognizing these situations you will easily be able to overcome these urges. Usually these cravings have "triggers" that are in our environment or inside of ourselves.

People, things, certain places can be triggers and remind you of drinking. These are easily controllable and avoidable. The triggers that sometimes come from "the inside" are more complex. You can suddenly find a longing to drink come up from nowhere. An emotion, a thought or a memory can suddenly build up an urge for having a drink.

So how to avoid these triggers? Well one of the most obvious one is do not keep alcohol at your home. That's a given. Try to stay away from situations that involve drinking. Turn down invitations to parties or gatherings that you know will have alcohol. The key here is temporary. This is not for life. Just while you are getting your things together. In the future you can slowly start to incorporate the people, places or things into your life again (if that is what you want) without having the need to drink. If you feel bad about turning down an invitation remind yourself that it is nothing personal. Don't be co-dependent. Grown-ups will understand your situation. You friends will understand. Real ones at least. You could come up with an idea instead to meet them in another surrounding. Going for a hike or to the movies. It doesn't have to involve drinking.

It is important to know you weaknesses. If you feel like you have the urge to drink when the weekend is getting closer you have to re-act to it. Do something that takes your mind of it. Start thinking about weekends as a time to party and start to thinking about them as chance to do other things like jogging, hiking, walk in the park, meeting family, going to shows or to travel. Doing those things will fill your life and leave you with a good feeling inside. Drinking will only leave you with an empty feeling and guilty conscience.

Remember the past. If you feel like quitting and you want to have a drink then you have to remember why you decided to stop drinking. You may have a flashback to a good time involving alcohol and your old friends. You have to be aware of this and realize that this is your mind playing tricks on you. What it isn't telling you and reminding you of are the bad times, the headaches, the hangover and the bad moral after maybe having done something you would normally be too embarassed to do when sober.

Some of your friends will also encourage you to start drinking with them again. This is a big social pressure for most people and can be very hard to resist. This is a time when it is very important to you to have strength and courage to say no to them and you are changing your life and it's the most important thing in your life. These people can't accept that you have taken another road than they have and in many cases they envy you of this decision. Don't let this people control you or to affect your decision. What do you have to gain? What do you have to loose? While you maybe gain a short-lived time of fun with your old friends you may end up loosing your spouse, your family, your house and your piece of mind. So have the courage to say no to them - even if it means that they will say goodbye to you. You are the most important thing in this matter. Be true to yourself. Maybe your friends are afraid of loosing you and in that case it will be a good idea to arrange another meeting were you do something else together. Watch a game or go for a walk together. Let them know that this is nothing personal and you are not leaving them as a friend although you don't want to drink with them anymore.

Chapter 13: Medications For

Alcoholism Treatment

You have to realize that there is no "perfect treatment" that can magically get rid of your desire or need to drink. But the good news is that there are a number of medications approved by the FDA which doctors can prescribe to treat alcoholism. These medications can help in reducing insatiable cravings for alcohol and in considerably cutting back on the number of heaving drinking days. They are more effective when combined with social and psychological interventions like the AA 12 Step Program.

But you also need to note that in spite of the current understanding that alcoholism is actually a persistent medical condition, there are still some people who believe that alcohol dependence and abuse are moral failures which can be conquered by sheer willpower. But medical experts in addiction firmly believe that medications should not be considered as substitutes for drinking alcohol. Rather, medications should be prescribed to aid in making the difference between a successful recovery and relapse of an alcoholic. They can work best and be most effective when taken with psychosocial modalities. Currently, there are 3 drugs for the treatment of alcoholism that are FDA-approved. But there is also a 4th drug which has shown potential in recent clinical trials.

Antabuse

For more than 50 years now, Antabuse has been approved by the FDA to treat alcoholism. As such, it is considered as the oldest medication in the market for such purpose. Antabuse functions by restricting the ability of the body to absorb alcohol. In particular, it inhibits the production of a specific enzyme that allows the body to absorb acetaldehyde, which is a product of alcohol breakdown.

When your body has no enzyme to break acetaldehyde down, acetaldehyde will start to build up in your system even if you ingest a small amount of alcohol. This will then result in very unpleasant side effects such as palpitations, nausea and flushing. You can think of Antabuse as making you decide not to drink alcohol in order to prevent those side effects. Antabuse will not really get rid of our cravings to drink. You will still be able to get the "good effects" alcohol when you drink but eventually, you will reach a point when you will begin to feel sick. You can also think of Antabuse as sort of a "chaperone" for you when you go to social events where there will be alcoholic drinks. When you start feeling the side effects of the drug, you will know that it is time to stop so you will not have to get very sick.

Medical experts prefer to prescribe Antabuse when they know that its intake can be monitored – either at home by your spouse or other family member or in an alcoholism clinic. Some doctors have hesitations in prescribing Antabuse because it is contrary to what they believe is the best method of preventing relapse which is complete abstinence from alcohol.

Naltrexone

This medication aids in reducing both the pleasure that an alcoholic gets from alcohol and the cravings that pushes him or her to seek out more alcohol. Naltrexone is able to do so by inhibiting docking sites or receptors for endorphins in the brain and by blocking the proteins generated by the body that aid in elevating mood. Those specific brain receptors are the same ones that accept other drugs like heroin and morphine. Doctors typically prescribe Naltrexone to be taken one pill per day. But the FDA has recently approved the new once a month dosage of the injectable form.

Unlike Antabuse, naltrexone is able to address the very core of alcoholism or addiction. Alcoholism is basically a condition wherein when you drink alcohol; you want to drink more and more of it. When you start drinking only a couple of drinks, you will find it hard to stop even after drinking 10 or more drinks because you are pursuing the positive effects of alcohol. What Naltrexone does is break that positive feedback cycle so you can have a couple of drink and not crave for more.

Certain clinical trials have shown that oral naltrexone can aid in reducing the number of relapses to heavy drinking which is currently defined as 5 or more drinks per day for men and 4 or more drinks per day for women. In the Combining Medications and Behavioral Interventions for

Alcoholism or COMBINE which was funded by NIAAA or the National Institute on Alcohol Abuse and Alcoholism, it was revealed that naltrexone can be effectively used in treating alcoholism up to twenty sessions of alcohol counseling a behavioral expert. It is important for naltrexone to be administered under the close supervision of a doctor.

Many doctors now prefer Vivitrol, which is the once-a-month injectable form of naltrexone; because it allows patients to better stick with a medication that they only have to take on a monthly basis.

Campral

Campral is a medication that is orally taken 3 times per day. The medication primarily acts in the brain's chemical messenger systems. It is also known to lessen the following alcohol withdrawal symptoms: restlessness, anxiety, insomnia and unpleasant mood changes that can result in relapse. Different research studies and clinical trials conducted in Europe have shown that regular intake of Campral can increase a patient's chances of refraining from drinking for a number of weeks or even months.

But certain research studies conducted in the United States and a COMBINE clinical trial show that there are no clear benefits from using Campral, whether taken with naltrexone or taken alone. But it has also been reported that the patients involved in the clinical trials in Europe were more severely depended on alcohol compared to the patients involved in the U.S. research studies. It has also been reported that the majority of the patients involved in the European clinical studies have abstained from drinking for longer periods of time prior to taking Campral. The NIAAA said that these two factors can account for the variances in the results.

Topamax

The FDA has actually approved Topamax for seizure treatment but not really for alcoholism treatment. Topamax has the same functionalities as Campral and can also help alcoholics the same way by avoiding or reducing the symptoms linked to long-term abstinence from alcohol.

Medications alone are not enough to treat alcoholism.

The above medications are most effective when taken as part of a psychosocial treatment. They are not really considered effective when taken alone. There are basically 3 types of psychosocial therapy that experts have considered very effective for alcoholism treatment. All of them have approximately the same success rates.

Cognitive behavioral therapy. It is a type of psychotherapy that focuses on the identification and modification of thought patterns and negative thoughts.

12 step facilitation. A popular example is Alcoholics Anonymous wherein patients are encouraged to undergo a 12-step program.

Motivational enhancement therapy. This approach is considered patient-centered wherein a counselor will attempt to get you to ponder and convey your motivations for change and help you in developing a personal plan that can help you in making the required changes.

Chapter 14: Dealing With Peer

Pressure

Peer pressure, while being seen as something only preteens to young adult's face, can be very common and very subtle. It all depends on what is said to a particular kind of person and when.

Here's what I mean: If a senior high school boy were to talk to a freshman girl, so her friends were no longer next to her (they kept moving while she was stopped) and said, "Hey, do you want a drink?" ... What would you say happened next?

Not everyone will succumb to this type of pressure. Some people are very strong-willed and will do anything they can in order to stand up for their beliefs. But once someone is in a new environment and they feel like the ground they are could shake and push them down at any moment, they're more likely to do what they can to fit in to reestablish some firmer ground and stand amongst the crowd.

But most people, especially those who are very young and gaining insecurity the more they are told about their "future roles" ("To be a good wife, please your husband." "Man up, stop looking weak." "You'll be in charge of this someday."). It puts a lot of pressure on a young individual with a still easily transformable mind to fit into a certain mold in society or become an outcast and never have someone care for you again.

Yes, it seems dramatic, but that's the reality of how they feel in these positions. Humans crave affection and to have a social circle. We can literally die from a lack of touch as babies, and our health can actually decline with no type of touch in a day, so it is necessary for many reasons. It is a survival instinct coded within our genes to search out others and bond with them. Even as adults, we still get these same types of thoughts running through our brain because of how we are coded to function.

So how is someone supposed to handle peer pressure, especially those who are more likely to say "Yes" to whatever someone asks or those who aren't good alone in social situations?

Go to an event with those you trust

You can trust a lot of people, but the type of people I am referring to here are the ones who you can stick close to during a party or social event and won't be pressured into doing anything. A simple "yes" or "no" question may be asked, but they'll respect your opinion. They also won't leave you on your own (if you're in a group; in a pair, it's more likely to happen if you both want to do separate things).

Stay around those similar to you

I don't mean those who act or talk in the same way. I mean those who have the same goals as you. In this case, this may be to stick with the designated drivers or others who aren't drinking at a particular event. They'll not only keep you company, but now you'll have a distraction from drinking, a declined urge to drink, and people to laugh at all of the drunken activities with. Let's be honest, some people are wild when they drink. There's always going to be one interesting thing happening in a gathering with enough alcohol to make someone drunk.

Build up your self-esteem and confidence

This will take a lot more time and effort to build up if you don't have enough of it already. But being confident in your choices and decisions can help you to be able to stand up for yourself when someone asks you to do something you don't want to do. So, if someone asks you for a drink or insists you should drink, having confidence can help you to say, "No thanks, I don't want one," and walk away if needed.

Walking away from a group when this can take substantial amounts of courage, but it is also probably one of the most helpful things to do when dealing with peer pressure. Getting out of the situation you feel pressured, no matter what you are being pressured to do in this social setting, should always take precedence over the other person's feelings.

The one exception to this is you may like it, which could become dangerous quickly. In which case, you should attract the attention of those nearby you by speaking more loudly, making eye contact with someone, repeating a phrase over and over ("No, I don't want to do that, please stop asking"), and, if needed, make a scene. This may not happen as often with alcohol itself, but there can be this pressure on people, especially females, to drinks to get drunk so the person can take advantage of you. Again, many advantages to being in a group and being confident here.

Building them up will also help you with many another aspect of your identity and daily life! Feeling more confidence will you be more comfortable in your skin and make you feel like you can move more freely throughout the world. It will give you the courage to ask out someone, apply for a job you aren't totally sure if you'll land, and to ask for a promotion or pay raise in some cases!

Being able to stick up for yourself because you are confident in how you move about the world is important to stand up for this culture or tearing another down to raise yourself up. Lift others up with you so you can all be happier and more confident people than you were before.

Look for the lies

This applies mainly to those who are younger, but if anyone ever says, "Everyone does this thing by now!" ... Definitely an exaggeration. There are too many people for everyone to be doing the same exact thing. This type of statement can make someone feel like it is better to go with what is being forced upon them because of this.

But remember to stand your ground. Don't feel any less because "every" one of your peers is doing something. The reality is that people are lying to seem cooler or older than they are in some of these types of situations. Sure, maybe almost everyone at a party is drinking some alcohol. Doesn't mean they're getting completely wasted or having anything super hard like vodka. It's common to mix drinks up a bit or to even have a small amount of alcohol followed by another drink, like water or soda.

Another way to see if there is a lie in this particular type of scenario: see how drunk the other is. If someone insists you drink, but you don't see a cup for themselves, that's a red flag to definitely not accept that cup. If they are completely drunk and insisting you drink, that's probably because they also want another drink and think everyone should be having a drink.

Chapter 15: Treatments For Alcohol Use Disorder

Alcohol use disorder is what doctors call it when you can't control how much you drink and have trouble controlling and managing your feelings when you're not drinking. A lot of people think the only way to control the disorder is through willpower as if it's a problem they can to resolve independently.

But alcohol use disorder is a brain disease, it affects the mind, which will make quitting difficult. And wanting to home-treat it could be difficult and insufficient.

An important step is to get more information about your treatment option, you will find lots of them to choose from.

Focus on your Doctor

Alcoholism (not a medical term) is some sort of alcohol use disorder. E.g, when people misuse alcohol but aren't dependent on it.

A medical doctor may say you have alcohol use disorder if you:

Think everyone else needs to drink.

Can't control your drinking habit.

Look miserable when you don't drink.

When you talk to your doctor, discuss your problems and goals. Do you need to drink less or stop it co mpletely? Together, you can come up with a treatment plan. Your doctor might also refer you to treatment experts who can help.

Treatment Options

Often, the best treatment for you depends on your circumstances as well as your goals. Most people look for a combination of very effective treatments, and you can get by booking for a visit with your doctor who will explain to you your best treatment option. Getting effective treatment mostly requires that you are admitted into a rehab or hospital for a while. There are other treatment plans where you can be an outpatient, by getting help from the nearest rehab center to your home..

See a doctor

For people who have severe alcohol use disorder, it is the most important step. The goal is to stop drinking and give your body ample time to drain the alcohol out of your body. It might take days or weeks.

Most people visit the hospital or rehab to get help for symptoms like:

Shaking (tremors)

Seeing or perceiving things that aren't real (hallucinations).

Seizures

Doctors and other experts could keep a eye you and prescribe medication in relations to the symptoms you're exhibiting.

Visit a Counselor or Therapist

With alcohol use disorder, controlling your drinking helps a great deal. Also, you should attempt to learn new skills and ways of doing things daily. Psychologists, social employees, or alcohol consumption counselors can show you how to:

Change your thoughts towards drinks.

Cope with stress and other triggers.

Get a support system.

Write down your goals and reach them.

A lot of people need a short, and intense counseling program. Others may want one-on-one therapy for a longer time to handle issues like stress or depression. Alcohol can have a great influence on people close to you, so partner or family therapy might help too.

Medications

No medicine can "treat" alcohol use disorder; however, many might help as you recover. They can make drinking less fun, so you don't enjoy doing it often.

Disulfiram (Antabuse) could make you feel sick when you drink.

Acamprosate (Campral) might help with urges.

Naltrexone (Revia) blocks the high feeling you get from drinking.

Drugs used for other conditions like smoking, pain, or epilepsy can also be associated with alcohol use disorder.

Consult your doctor to find out which of these plans suit you best.

Join a Group

Group therapy or a support group might help during rehabilitation and assist you to stick to instructions as life gets back to normal.

Group therapy led by a therapist, can offer you get the best of treatment combined with the support gotten from other users. Therapists don't influence organizations; instead, they are a group of people who have overcome alcohol use disorder; for instance, Alcoholics Anonymous, wise recovery, and other programs. Your group can be understanding and provide advice and help you keep up with responsiblilty. Many people remain in groups like this for a very long time.

What to Expect

Recovery might take a long time, so you may need continuous treatment. Several people in recovery do relapse and drink again, however, not everyone who has remained sober for at least a year relapse.

If you do, don't start to think you've failed. It's a step to recovery, and it makes recovery easy. After five years, only one out of seven people have difficulties with drinks. Treatment can work -- give yourself time.

Chapter 16: Control Center

This is your new control center. Your center of operations. Once you're there, see how long you can stay there, even while continuing the day's activities. Practice following your own instructions; doing only the things you'd have yourself do as a personal project. The way you'd visualize a perfect day. Will you clean the house? Will you go for a jog? Wash the car? This is all up to you. All I know for sure is you won't drink. Because as long as you stay in the control center; as long as you trust your own, best advice; as long as you dismiss the distant complaints of the ego, you will not act against yourself. As long as you stay in this place, ego dismissed, it will have no power over you. In this place, you are physically separated from the very germ that gave you alcoholism. Here, you are cured.

As in any mental ailment, a psychiatrist will seek to find the root cause. This is what we've done. We've sought and found the addiction at its source, right smack in the middle of the ego. The others will struggle; even those who don't drink a drop for the rest of their lives by will power alone, will be perpetually at odds with their own egos. You will not. You've gotten to the root of the problem; you've seen how it works, and most importantly, you can differentiate its voice from the voice of your best interests. That done, let's return to the beam in thine eye. It's time to take your own advice. It's time to take control of your life. Now, what would you have yourself do?

The amazing answer to this question is: anything you want. Anything good. Anything useful. But poison your body? Put sugar in your gas tank? Why would you? Why did you ever? It doesn't matter anymore. Because now that you're in the control center, it's no longer an issue. In this place of reason; composure; control; you have complete and total power over what you do.

This process is something that needs to be *felt* to make total sense, not simply read about in a book. For this reason, I'm going to describe what it feels like the best I can, and hope that it resonates with you.

Picture this. Pretend you're playing a video game. A role-playing video game. Where you take a character and lead him through his journey, building up his statistics, learning new skills, and progressing towards his goal. This character simply does what you tell him to. He responds to your controls. With no ego to contend with, he simply obeys your every command.

Depending on your affinity for video games, this may or may not be a good metaphor. Personally, as a child of the 80s, I can really identify with it. It makes the most sense to me, and it's the hand-rail I personally use how to keep myself on track.

In my daily life, I give my ego no chance to get in the way of doing what keeps me sober, happy, and healthy. I like to think of my own control center as a big cozy easy chair with a video game controller. As I sit there reclining in my own brain, it's as if I'm controlling my body with this video game controller. Since I'm the one in charge of my body now; at the helm of my own control center, I can make myself do all sorts of great stuff I would never have had the discipline to do in the past. At this very moment, I'm driving to the gym after a grueling, twelve-hour shift at work, dictating this chapter into my phone. My ego would never have allowed this. My ego would punish the very idea of this with feelings of dread, of exhaustion, of pain, and of general "Hell no, there's no way we're going to the gym to do squats right now, that would totally suck. Let's go home and crack a beer instead."

And in fact, that's exactly what I'm doing right now. And I'm doing it with no sense of dread, no feeling of anxiety, no tiredness, no weariness, and absolutely no doubt in myself. Before I adopted this system of thinking, there would be absolutely *no way* I'd be going to work out right now. No way I'd be writing this book either. I'd be going directly home to open a beer; a character controlled by my ego, not by my me. So tell me: which one of us is controlling me right now? My lazy, alcoholic ego, or me? And as long as I have the controller in *my* hands, I am the one in control.

If it suits you, try to picture yourself doing the exact same thing. With your ego out of the way, picture yourself in your own mental easy chair, having stepped back from the big bubble of your ego and sitting down comfortably. You are now in your own control center. Pick up the controller. You are now in control. Unhindered and unburdened by your own ego, take inventory of this character you're controlling right now. What is his current state? What has he been doing wrong up until now? And most importantly, what would you have him do from now on? Now that you've cast the beam from thine own eye; now that your earthly body is your own, personal project? What will you have your beloved character do?

You already know what's in his best interest. Trust yourself, and follow your own advice. The only thing that was keeping you from following your own advice was your ego, and with that out of the way, you are free to dictate your own actions. Not only are you able to ignore your ego's desire to drink, but you're free to improve in every area of your life. It's truly difficult to put into words the sense of freedom you feel when the implications of this simple concept really sink in. I remember when it happened to me. All of a sudden, simply trusting myself, following my own directives without a negative emotion to be had, it occurred to me: "Wow. I can do absolutely anything I want." This was the moment for me that Dr. Lewis described when he wrote: "And that moment, when you switch sides and become your own coach, feels so right... that you already know it's going to work before the first day is over."

I'll never forget the moment that I realized I had become my own coach. I wrote this book because I want *you* to have that moment too. In summary, the system is this:

Recognize that your ego is the one keeping you from changing. Every pang of anxiety, every twinge of dread; these are all chemical functions of your brain, induced by a part of your psyche incapable of reasoning. This is why even though you know what's best for yourself, there's a force inside that has been keeping you from doing it.

Get a grip on your ego. Now that you've identified the culprit, use visualization to step outside of its influence. Find a place instead where you can use reasoning without interference.

Trust yourself! There is a higher power within all of us; one with all the right answers, yet we bend to the chemical impulses of the ego. Trust yourself, and follow your own good advice!

Established Facts:

The ego can only compel you, not control you. Recognize it for what it is, and its power over you will diminish.

Chapter 17: Join A Support Group

How each addict will recover from alcoholism is different, therapy might be the major factor for some, and it might as well be medication or simple lifestyle changes for others. However, if there is one factor playing winning the lottery more often than these other strategies. It's the help of support groups.

Support groups are many all around the world. Mostly, they are made up of recovered alcoholics for struggling alcoholics. Their goal is to help recovering alcoholics such as yourself to recover. Their doors are always open and most times membership requires simply being an alcoholic who wishes to recover.

In this chapter, we will examine the two major support groups available around you that you can join right away.

Alcoholics Anonymous

Alcoholics Anonymous(AA) is the most popular support group in the world. Founded in 1935, it is an international mutual aid fellowship with the aim of keeping its members sober and helping new members achieve sobriety. It is a nonprofit, non-professional supporting group and the requirement for members is the desire to stop drinking.

Since 1935 that it was founded, other therapies such as drugs and behavioral therapies have been invented for alcoholism. But alcoholic anonymous members still report higher success rates, especially when members combine other therapies such as medications and therapy with AA meetings. So the cost-free AA is still the best way out to many.

The big book and the 12 steps

AA was found in 1935 after a recovered alcoholic, Billy Wilson talked to another alcoholic, Bob Smith about the habit of alcoholism and possible solutions. This lead to the first support group being formed with the help of other early members.

In the year 1939, the book Alcoholics Anonymous: The story of how more than 100 have recovered from alcoholism was published. The book title became the name of the organization and the book is largely referred to as "the Big Book" till this present moment.

It is called the book because the first edition contained 164 pages, and it's been virtually unchanged since then. The big book proposes a 12-step program in which members admit that they are powerless over alcohol and need help from a "higher power".

Members seek strength and willpower through prayers, meditation and reading the Bible to listen to God's voice or worship a higher power of their own making. The other steps include making moral inventory to include resentments and a list of character defects, listing mistakes and preparing to make amends, and the final step is to try to help others recover.

The original twelve steps as published in the Big book is;

1) We admitted we were powerless over alcohol—that our lives had become unmanageable.

2) Came to believe that a power greater than ourselves could restore us to sanity.

3) Made a decision to turn our will and our lives over to the care of God as we understood Him.

4) Made a searching and fearless moral inventory of ourselves.

5) We admit to God, to ourselves, and to another human being the exact nature of our wrongs.

6) We are entirely ready to have God remove all these defects of character.

7) Humbly asked God to remove our shortcomings.

8) We made a list of all persons we had harmed and became willing to make amends to them all.

9) We have made direct amends to such people wherever possible, except when to do so would injure them or others.

10) We have continued to take personal inventory, and when we were wrong, promptly admitted it.

11) Sought through prayer and meditation to improve our conscious contact with

God as we understood Him, praying only for knowledge of His will for us and the power to carry that out.

12) Having had a spiritual awakening as the result of these steps, we tried to carry this message to alcoholics and to practice these principles in all our affairs.

This 12 step is the guiding principle of AA meetings. The beauty of AA is that it's everywhere. It has spread across diverse cultures holding different beliefs and views, including regions that frown on non-governmental and nonprofit movements. Millions of people around the world attend AA meetings yearly, so you won't find it hard to find a group.

Even though AA sounds like a religious cult and the Big book makes reference to God, it's not a religious organization. They only adopt a spiritual nature because of the needed atmosphere of transcendence but they also hold a flexible worldview so people from different backgrounds can feel at ease in their meetings.

Members may interpret the idea of higher power any way they like, and anonymity is promoted - first names only. Membership is free and maintenance cost is maintained by voluntary contributions.

The group's program goes far beyond quitting alcohol. The major aim of the big book is to promote a total mindset shift or what is called a spiritual awakening. A spiritual awakening is aimed to be achieved after completing the 12 steps and further complemented by attending AA meetings and volunteering.

Sponsors

New members are encouraged to find a sponsor to help them with the 12 steps and their recovery. A sponsor is a recovered alcoholic with the concrete experience of the 12 steps. They are usually the same sex as their charges and refrain from imposing their personal views on their charges.

A sponsor's role is to guide the new member through the steps while also integrating him or her into the community. And it is a win-win situation because the sponsors themselves benefit from the relationship because as they help others stop drinking, they themselves reduce their tendency of relapsing. It's also a win for the new members because they receive free moral support, advice and a model to emulate.

Meeting and How it helps

AA members agree that they have a disease and refer to themselves as alcoholics. They usually discuss alcoholism exclusively in their meetings.

Their most common type of meeting involves each member sharing their personal stories and experiences with the 12 steps one by one and their efforts to meet the challenge of recovery. As a new member, you will be urged to attend daily for the first few months, because that's when the urge to relapse is greatest.

Don't refuse to do it because you are scared of sharing. There is no obligation in AA, members are perfectly accommodating, and they won't impose rules on you. You are free to attend and gain in any way you can until you are free to share.

The meetings are usually therapeutic sessions run by alcoholics for alcoholics. There is often no clear instructor or student, members are just there to share and help each other. But this doesn't mean AA groups have no structure.

They have several types of meetings. There are closed meetings in which only alcoholics willing to change are allowed in. There are open meetings where everyone (both alcoholics and non-alcoholics) is free to come in and listen. There are speaker meetings in which one or more members come in from neighborhood AA groups to share their experiences.

There are Big book meetings in which members take a turn reading from the big book and then discussing how they relate to what they read. There are 12 step meetings in which members form several subgroups and each work on the 12 steps based on which stage they are in their spiritual awakening.

AA is also a fellowship in all forms of the word. It serves as a substitute for social drinking. If you are fond of drinking due to boredom, AA takes that tendency away.

As a new member, you make new friends and learn new ways to cope with cravings. With the help of your friends and sponsor, you work to overcome your addiction by following the 12 steps to the best of your ability.

There is no judgment in AA and their slogan " One day at a time" serves as a reminder that relapses are to be expected.

Also, listening to others share their experiences helps you realize that you are not alone in your struggle and you actually correct a lot of your misconception from others' experiences. In time, as you grow more experienced and have overcome your addiction. You are urged to become a sponsor that helps others too.

SMART groups

Smart stands for Self-Management and Recovery Training. The Smart system is a science-based group and makes use of CBT and Rational Emotional Behavioral Therapy (REBT) techniques rather than motivational methods. The tools and techniques taught in smart meetings are based on scientific research aimed at helping members make better life choices, and not on the 12 steps used by Alcoholics Anonymous.

SMART groups are different in that they don't encourage members to endorse powerlessness or the need for a higher power. They don't label alcoholism as a disease either. They see it as a dysfunctional habit and members learn skills to deal with their cravings and urges for the long term.

Method

SMART groups are based on scientific knowledge and the techniques used are constantly updated due to evaluations of members. The program is based on CBT and REBT techniques as well as other validated psychological research on treatment.

The key focus of SMART support groups is self-reliance and self-empowerment.

With the aid of trained volunteers, new members are taught self-reliance to control their addictive behaviors and how to examine one's behavior so as to determine the problems that warrant the most attention.

Some of the topics covered includes

1) Replacing impulsive self-destructive thoughts with rational self-motivating thoughts

2) Setting achievable goals and milestones throughout the recovery process.

3) Accepting impulses as part of the process and accounting for them.

4) Learning to resist urges and cravings

5) Learning patience and how to start again after relapsing

6) Learning self-responsibility and self-discipline by taking discrete action throughout the recovery process.

In smart meetings, relapses are not seen as a failure of the process. In fact, meetings focus more on relapses as an opportunity to review what happened and how to get back on track. Therefore, recognizing relapses as a mistake, rather than a failure helps members maintain their motivation throughout recovery.

The SMART 4 Point Program

SMART support groups' methods are based on a four-point system. Each aspect of the programs help you as a new member to build a new sober and healthy lifestyle. However, it's important to know that it's not a step program. Because new members are made to tackle each point according to their needs.

Point 1 - Building And Maintaining motivation

There will always be temptations to drink. The first point is about building a source of motivation. You are urged to make a list of priorities and consider the adverse effects of your drinking habits on your life and long-term goals. You are also taught to seek out motivation by discussing your habit with your loved ones, attending counseling session and talking to other recovering alcoholics.

Point 2 - Coping with urges

The second point helps you recognize urges and how to cope with them. You will learn how to cope with cravings with specific mental and behavioral methods. Methods include finding distractions, avoiding alcohol-related events, staying away from potential triggers and spending time with other smart members.

Point 3 - Managing Thoughts, Feelings, and Behaviors

The third point is all about replacing your negative mindset with positive and self-motivating thoughts. Recovery is difficult so you are urged to talk better to yourself instead of beating yourself down all the time which is the cause of depression. You are taught to accept yourself and your life experiences so you can move forward. You are also taught strategies to examine your thought process so you can eradicate irrational and unreasonable thoughts urging you to drink.

Point 4 - Living A Balanced life

This point tackles how to live without alcohol. You are urged to make a list of priorities, activities, and routines that will form your new lifestyle. You are taught a realistic goal setting and how to plan for the future.

Smart recovery can be used as single based treatments but members are advised not to. About 50 percent of members combine regular meeting attendance with other therapies such as AA, psychotherapy, and medications.

Meeting and Graduations

Smart meetings take place all around the world in physical destinations and online and are completely free for everyone wishing to attend. The cost of maintenance is paid by voluntary donations by attending members.

It is extremely beneficial to members and it's the biggest competition for AA. You are urged to attend 5 sessions before you decide if it's a perfect fit for you. This gives you enough time to learn more about the group and socialize with other members of the group.

Group meetings consist more of teaching sessions in which experienced volunteering members hand out resources and teach techniques that can help new members with each point of the program. Members can also share their experiences, especially their mistakes and relapses. Experienced members then share strategies on how to change for the better.

The support groups are also there so you make new friends and these friends offer moral support on your journey.

However, one distinguishing factor of SMART groups is that it's not lifelong and you can graduate. They operate with stages and once you reach the final stage, you are considered as having all the necessary skills of leading a sober life.

The stages include;

Precontemplation stage – At this stage, the group realizes that you may not know that you have a drinking problem.

Contemplation stage – At this stage, you start to evaluate the advantages and disadvantages of the addiction by weighing the cost against the benefits

Determination stage – At this stage, you try to pursue personal change, and but usually fail on your own.

Action stage - at this stage, you seek out new ways of handling your addiction behavior. This can include self-help, the support of addiction help group or professional guidance.

Maintenance stage– After a few months, your behavior has changed and you now seek to maintain this newfound sobriety.

Graduation stage – Once a participant has sustained a long period of change, the group believes that one may choose to move on with their lives and "graduate" from SMART Recovery.

Family and friends

SMART support groups are not only beneficial to recovering addicts alone. They also open their doors to the family and friends associated with the negative side effects of your drinking.

SMART groups believe that alcoholism can have severe side effects on the professional and personal life of the addict's loved ones. Smart recovery groups help to educate these families and friends on how to better communicate and support their loved ones having the drinking problem.

They learn how to provide encouragement in time of need, while also recovering from the bad habits of the alcoholic. Family members and friends can attend these special group meetings for as long as they want and can also come back to check up on the group, give updates and find solutions to new challenges.

Conclusion

I hope that I was able to help you discover what alcohol addiction is and what you can to do next to eliminate it once and for all. The problem is that unless you admit that you have a problem, people around you are going to suffer. Do you want to lose your loved ones? You may not already know it, but the booze is gradually alienating people that you love who can't cope with the self-destructive course that you have decided to take in your life. You have to do something now, or you may lose them.

Well, the next step is to start implementing the suggestions I've given in this book so that you can enjoy a much more satisfying and joyful life.

The problem is that people who drink alcohol on a hefty basis are often in a world which isn't quite real. They don't blame themselves when things go wrong. They look for excuses. It's time to face up to the fact that you have a problem because until you do, you can't even start to find a solution.

Thank you and good luck!

CPSIA information can be obtained
at www.ICGtesting.com
Printed in the USA
BVHW042035020521
606221BV00017B/1586